History

ROBERT LOWELL

HISTORY

FARRAR, STRAUS AND GIROUX

NEW YORK

8 | 1 . 5

Note

About 80 of the poems in *History* are new, the
rest are taken from my last published poem,
Notebook begun six years ago. All the poems
have been changed, some heavily. I have
plotted. My old title, *Notebook*, was more
accurate than I wished, i.e. the composition
was jumbled. I hope this jumble or jungle is
cleared—that I have cut the waste marble from
the figure.

c. 1

For Frank Bidart
and Stanley Kunitz

Contents

15

16

17

18

19

20

History

History

History has to live with what was here,
clutching and close to fumbling all we had—
it is so dull and gruesome how we die,
unlike writing, life never finishes.
Abel was finished; death is not remote,
a flash-in-the-pan electrifies the skeptic,
his cows crowding like skulls against high-voltage wire,
his baby crying all night like a new machine.
As in our Bibles, white-faced, predatory,
the beautiful, mist-drunken hunter's moon ascends—
a child could give it a face: two holes, two holes,
my eyes, my mouth, between them a skull's no-nose—
O there's a terrifying innocence in my face
drenched with the silver salvage of the mornfrost.

Man and Woman

The sheep start galloping in moon-blind wheels
shedding a dozen ewes—is it faulty vision?
Will we get them back . . . and everything,
marriage and departure, departure and marriage,
village to family, family to village—
all the sheep's parents in geometric progression?
It's too much heart-ache to go back to that—
not life-enhancing like the hour a student
first discovers the unblemished Mother
on the Tuscan hills of Berenson,
or of Galileo, his great glass eye
admiring the spots on the erroneous moon. . . .
I watch this night out grateful to be alone
with my wife—your slow pulse, my outrageous eye.

Bird?

Adrift in my sweet sleep . . . I hear a voice
singing to me in French, "*O mon avril.*"
Those nasals . . . they woo us. Spring. Not mine. Not mine. . . .
A large pileated bird flies up,
dropping excretions like a frightened snake
in Easter feathers; its earwax-yellow spoonbill
angrily hitting the air from side to side
blazing a passage through the smothering jungle—
the lizard tyrants were killed to a man by this bird,
man's forerunner. I picked up stones, and hoped
to snatch its crest, the crown, at last, and cross
the perilous passage, sound in mind and body . . .
often reaching the passage, seeing my thoughts
stream on the water, as if I were cleaning fish.

Dawn

The building's color is penny-postcard pale
as new wood—thirty stories, or a hundred?
The distant view-windows glisten like little cells;
on a wafer balcony, too thin to sit on,
a crimson blazer hangs, a replica
of my own from Harvard—hollow, blowing,
shining its Harvard shield to the fall air. . . .
Eve and Adam, adventuring from the ache
of the first sleep, met forms less primitive
and functional, when they gazed on the stone-ax
and Hawaiian fig-leaf hanging from their fig-tree. . . .
Nothing more established, pure and lonely,
than the early Sunday morning in New York—
the sun on high burning, and most cars dead.

In Genesis

Blank. A camel blotting up the water.
God with whom nothing is design or intention.
In the Beginning, the Sabbath could last a week,
God grumbling secrecies behind Blue Hill. . . .
The serpent walked on foot like us in Eden;
glorified by the perfect Northern exposure,
Eve and Adam knew their nakedness,
a discovery to be repeated many times . . .
in joyless stupor? . . . Orpheus in Genesis
hacked words from brute sound, and taught men English,
plucked all the flowers, deflowered all the girls
with the overemphasis of a father.
He used too many words, his sons killed him,
dancing with grateful gaiety round the cookout.

Our Fathers

That cloud of witnesses has flown like nightdew
leaving a bundle of debts to the widow and orphan—
the virus crawling on its belly like a blot,
an inch an aeon; the tyrannosaur,
first carnivore to stand on his two feet,
the neanderthal, first anthropoid to laugh—
we lack staying power, though we will to live.
Abel learned this falling among the jellied
creepers and morning-glories of the saurian sunset.
But was there some shining, grasping hand to guide
me when I breathed through gills, and walked on fins
through Eden, plucking the law of retribution from the tree?
Was the snake in the garden, an agent provocateur?
Is the Lord increased by desolation?

Walks

In those days no *casus belli* to fight the earth
for the familial, hidden fundamental—
on their walks they scoured the hills to find a girl,
tomorrow promised the courage to die content.
The willow stump put out thin wands in leaf,
green, fleeting flashes of unmerited joy;
the first garden, each morning . . . the first man—
birds laughing at us from the distant trees,
troubadours of laissez-faire and love.
Conservatives only want to have the earth,
the great beast clanking its chain of vertebrae. . . .
Am I a free man, if I have no servant?
If at the end of the long walk, my old dog dies of joy
when I sit down, a poor man at my fire?

King David Old

Two or three times a night, and for a month,
we wrang the night-sweat from his shirt and sheets;
on the fortieth day, we brought him Abishag,
and he recovered, and he knew her not—
cool through the hottest summer day, and moist;
a rankness more savage than all the flowers,
as if her urine caused the vegetation,
Jerusalem leaping from the golden dew;
but later, the Monarch's well-beloved shaft
lay quaking in place; men thought the world was flat,
yet half the world was hanging on each breast,
as two spent swimmers that did cling together—
Sion had come to Israel, if they had held. . . .
This clinch is quickly broken, they were glad to break.

Solomon's Wisdom

"Can I go on keeping a hundred wives at fifty,
still scorning my aging and dispirited life
what I loved with wild idealism young?
God only deals a king one hand to gamble,
his people chosen for him and means to lie.
I shiver up vertical like a baby pigeon,
palate-sprung for the worm, senility.
I strap the gross artillery to my back,
lash on destroying what I lurch against,
not with anger, but unwieldy feet—
ballooning like a spotted, warty, blow-rib toad,
King Solomon croaking, *This too is vanity;*
her lips are a scarlet thread, her breasts are towers—
hymns of the terrible organ in decay."

Solomon, the Rich Man in State

While still man, he drank the fruits of the world,
from the days of his youth to the night of death;
but here the matching of his fresh-cut flowers
is overdelicate and dead for death,
and his flowery coverlet lies like lead
asserting that no primitive ferment,
the slobbering poignance of the voyeur God,
will soil the wise man's earthly abandoned vestment
spread like King Solomon in the Episcopal morgue,
here at earth's end with nowhere else to go—
still sanguine, fit to serve a thousand wives,
a heaven that held the gaze of Babylon.
So calm perhaps will be our final change,
won from the least desire to have what is.

Old Wanderer

A nomad in many cities, yet closer than I
to the grace of 19th century Europe,
to the title of the intellectuals
boiling in Dostoyevsky's Petersburg—
more German than Germans, most Jewish of Jews, a critic
who talked—too much, and never stayed with a subject,
a small Jewish gentleman disliking Jews—
the ancient wailing wanderer in person.
Like Marx you like to splatter the Liberal Weeklies
with gibing multilingual communiqués
shooting like Italians all the birds that fly.
You voice your mother's anxious maternal warnings,
but it's no use humoring anyone who says
we'll sleep better under a red counterpane than a green.

Judith

"The Jews were much like Arabs, I learned at Radcliffe,
decay of infeud scattered our bright clans;
now ours is an airier aristocracy:
professors, solons, new art, old, New York
where only Jews can write an English sentence,
the Jewish mother, half Jew, half anti-Jew,
says, *literate, liberalize, liberate!*
If her husband dies and takes his lay in state,
she calms the grandeur of his marble hair.
Like Judith, she'd cut the Virgin Mary dead,
A jet-set parachute. Long before the Philistines,
Jewish girls could write: for Judith, knowing
Holofernes was like knocking out a lightweight—
smack! her sword divorces his codshead from the codspiece."

Israel 1

The vagabond Alexander passed here, *romero*—
did he make Israel Greek, or just Near East?
This province, still provincial, prays to the One God
who left his footmark on the field of blood;
his dry wind bleeds the overcharged barbed wires. . . .
Wherever the sun ferments our people from dust,
our blood leaps up in friendship a cold spring. . . .
Alexander learned to share the earth with God;
God learned to live in a heaven, wizened with distance,
a face thin as a sand-dollar in the pail of a child. . . .
Each year some prince of tyrants, King Ahab, says,
"If my enemies could only know me, I am safe."
But the good murderer is always blind;
the leopard enters the Ark and keeps his spots.

Israel 2

The sun still burns in Israel. I could have stayed there
a month longer and even stood conscription,
though almost a pacifist, and still unsure
if Arabs are black . . . no Jew, and thirty years
too old. I loved the country, her briskness, danger,
jolting between salvation and demolition. . . .
Since Moses, the long march over, saw the Mountain
lift its bullet-head past timberline to heaven:
the ways of Israel's God are military;
from X to X, the prophets, unto Marx;
reprisal and terror, voices benumbed in noise;
finally, no one tells us which is which . . .
till arms fuse and sand reverts to chemical,
semper idem and ubique, our God of Hosts.

30

Israel 3

Morale and teamsoul are hardly what we market
back home; it makes us tired to batter our old car
stalled on the crossroads, heads in, both headlights on
yacking directives like Julius Caesar's missiles.
We have no forum for Roman rhetoricians—
even doubt, the first American virtue,
has drawbacks, it can't cure anything.
Time's dissolutions leave no air to breathe. . . .
Israel is all it had to be, a garrison;
spend ten days there, or as I, three weeks,
you find the best and worst of countries . . . glass,
faith's icicle-point sharpened till invisible.
God finds his country as He always will . . .
nowhere easier than Israel to stand up.

Helen

"I am the azure! come from the underworld,
I hear the serene erosion of the surf;
once more I see our galleys bleed with dawn,
lancing on muffled oarlocks into Troy.
My loving hands recall the absent kings,
(I used to run my fingers through their beards)
Agamemnon drowned in Clytemnestra's bath, Ulysses,
the great gulf boiling sternward from his keel. . . .
I hear the military trumpets, all their brass,
blasting the rhythm to the frantic oars,
the rowers' metronome enchains the sea.
High on beaked vermillion prows, the gods,
their fixed archaic smiles smarting with salt,
reach out carved, indulgent arms to me."

31

Achilles to the dying Lykaon

"Float with the fish, they'll clean your wounds, and lick
away your blood, and have no care of you;
nor will your mother wail beside your pyre
as you swirl down the Skamander to the sea,
but the dark shadows of the fish will shiver,
lunge and snap Lykaon's silver fat.
Trojans, you will perish till I reach Troy—
you'll run in front, I'll scythe you down behind;
nor will your Skamander, though whirling and silver, save you,
though you kill sheep and bulls, and drown a thousand
one-hoofed horse, still living. You must die
and die and die and die and die—
till the blood of my Patroklos is avenged,
killed by the wooden ships while I was gone."

Cassandra 1

"Such clouds, rainbows, pink rainstorms, bright green hills,
churches coming and going through the rain,
or wrapped in pale greenish cocoons of mist—
so crazy I snapped my lighter to see the sun.
Famine's joy is the enjoyment. Who'll deny
the crash, delirious uterus living it up?
In the end we may see all things in a glance,
like speed-up reading; but tell me what is love?
I don't mind someone finding someone better—
I was doomed in Troy with my sister Polyxena
and Achilles who fought to their deaths through love—
Paris saw Achilles' vulnerable tendon . . .
a lover will always turn his back. Why did Paris
kill our sister with Achilles while he had her?"

Cassandra 2

"Nothing less needed than a girl shining a mirror
darkening with the foliage of May,
waiting the miracle of the polishing winds. . . .
I was not wise, or unique in any skill;
not unreasonably, Zeus became my enemy,
I knew God's shadow for the coming night;
I saw in the steam of the straw the barn would burn.
I did not wish to save myself by running.
Does Agamemnon lying in our blood remember
my pointed fingers painted with red ink,
the badge of my unfulfilled desire to be,
the happiness of the drop to die in the river—
how I, a slave, followed my king on the red carpet? . . .
The wave of the wineglass trembled to see me walk."

Orestes' Dream

"As I sleep, our saga comes out clarified:
why for three weeks mother toured the countryside,
buying up earthenware, big pots and urns,
barbarous potsherds, such as the thirsty first
archaeologists broke on their first digs . . . not *our* art—
kingly the clay, common the workmanship.
For three weeks mother's lover kept carving
chess-sets, green leaf, red leaf, as tall as urns,
modern Viking design for tribal Argos. . . .
When Agamemnon, my father, came home at last,
he was skewered and held bubbling like an ox,
his eyes crossed in the great strain of the heat—
my mother danced with a wicker bullshead by his urn.
Can I call the police against my own family?"

Clytemnestra 1

"After my marriage, I found myself in constant
companionship with this almost stranger I found
neither agreeable, interesting, nor admirable,
though he was always kind and irresponsible.
The first years after our first child was born,
his daddy was out at sea; that helped, I could bask
on the couch of inspiration and my dreams.
Our courtship was rough, his disembarkation
unwisely abrupt. I was animal,
healthy, easily tired; I adored luxury,
and should have been an extrovert; I usually
managed to make myself pretty comfortable. . . .
Well," she laughed, "we both were glad to dazzle.
A genius temperament should be handled with care."

Clytemnestra 2

"O Christmas tree, how green thy branches—our features
could only be the most conventional,
the hardwood smile, the Persian rug's abstraction,
the firelight dancing in the Christmas candles,
my unusual offspring with his usual scowl,
spelling the fifty feuding kings of Greece,
with a red, blue and yellow pencil. . . . I
am seasick with marital unhappiness—
I am become the eye of heaven, and hate
my husband swimming like vagueness, like a porpoise,
in the imperial purple of his heart. . . .
He now lies dead beneath the torches like a lion,
he is like the rich golden collection-plate,
O Christmas tree, how green thy branches were . . ."

Clytemnestra 3

No folly could secularize the sacred cow,
our Queen at sixty worked in bed like Balzac.
Sun, moon and stars lay hidden in the cornstalk,
where she moved she left her indelible sunset.
She had the lower jaw of a waterbuffalo,
the weak intelligence, the iron will.
In one night boys fell senile in her arms. . . .
Later, something unsavory took place:
Orestes, the lord of murder and proportion,
saw the tips of her nipples had touched her toes—
a population problem and bad art.
He knew the monster must be guillotined.
He saw her knees tremble and he enjoyed the sight,
knowing that Trojan chivalry was shit.

White Goddess

"I'm scratchy, I don't wear these torpedoes
spliced to my chest for you to lift and pose. . . .
As a girl, I had crushes on our Amazons;
after our ten hour hikes, I snorted ten hours
or more, I had to let my soul catch up—
men will never, I thought, catch up with such women. . . .
In the götterdämmerung of the Paris Opera,
I met my Goddess, a Gold Coast negro singing
Verdi's *Desdemona* in the ebbing gold.
When Othello strangled her, she died, then bowed,
saying with noble shyness, 'I appreciate
your co-operation with my shortcomings.
I wish you the love of God, and a friend . . .'
I never met a woman I couldn't make."

Iknaton and the One God

The mother-sobs of Hera who knows that any
woman must love her husband more than her,
constantly hated though inconstantly loved—
man thought twice about making marriage legal;
men triumphed, made a mangod; he was single,
a sapling who breathed refreshment from a flower,
its faded petals the color of fresh wood—
no tyrant, just a mediocre student,
his rule has the new broom and haste of the One God,
Iknaton with spikes of the gold sun in his hair.
The Jews found hope in his Egypt, the King's plan a small thing,
as if one were both drowning and swimming at the same time . . .
the *it-must-be* on the small child's grave:
"Say, Passerby, that man is born to die."

Aswan Dam

Had Pharaoh's servants slaved like Nasser's labor,
Egyptian manhood under Russian foremen,
the pyramid. . . . I saw the Russians and imagined
they did more tangible work in a day than all Egypt. . . .
Dr. Mohammed Abdullah Fattah al Kassas
fears the Dam will slow the downstream current,
dunes and sandbars no longer build up buffers
along the Delta and repulse the sea—
the Mediterranean will drown a million farms,
wild water hyacinths evaporate Lake Nasser,
snails with wormlike bloodflukes slide incurably
to poison five hundred miles of new canals. . . .
Rake-sailed boats have fished the fertile Nile;
Pharaoh's death-ship come back against the shore.

Down the Nile

Two in the afternoon. The restlessness.
Greek Islands. Maine. I have counted the catalogue
of ships down half its length, the beaks of the bowsprits. . . .
Yet sometimes the Nile is wet, and life's as painted:
those couples, one in love and marriage, swaying
their children and their slaves the height of children,
supple and gentle as giraffes or newts;
the waist still willowy, the paint still fresh;
decorum without conforming, no harness on
the woman, and no armor on her husband,
the red clay master with his feet of clay
catwalking lightly to his conquests, leaving
one model and dynasties of faithless copies—
we aging downstream faster than a scepter can check.

Sheep

But we must remember our tougher roots:
forerunners bent in hoops to the broiling soil,
until their backs were branded with the coin
of Alexander, God or Caesar—
as if they'd been stretched on burning chicken wire,
skin cooked red and hard as rusted tin
by the footlights of the sun—tillers of the desert!
Think of them, afraid of violence,
afraid of anything, timid as sheep
hidden in some casual, protective crevice,
held twelve dynasties to a burning-glass,
pressed to the levelled sandbreast of the Sphinx—
what were once identities simplified
to a single, indignant, collusive grin.

Sappho to a Girl

I set this man before the gods and heroes—
he sits all day before you face to face,
like a cardplayer. Your elbow brushes his elbow;
when you speak he hears you and your laughter
is water hurrying over the clear stones. . . .
If I see you a moment it's hollowness;
you are the fairest thing on this dark earth.
I cannot speak, I cannot see—
a dead whiteness trickling pinpricks of sweat.
I am greener than the greenest green grass—
I die. I can easily make you understand me—
a woman is seldom enslaved by what is best;
her servants, her children, the daily household ache—
the moon slides west, the Pleiades; I sleep alone.

The Spartan Dead at Thermopylae

A friend or wife is usually right I think
in her particular fear, though not in general—
who told the Spartans at Thermopylae
that their death was coming with the dawn?
That morning Xerxes poured wine to the rising sun . . .
in his army many men, but few soldiers,
it was not a god who threatened Greece but man. . . .
Leonidas and his three hundred hoplites
glittering with liberation, combed one another's
golden Botticellian hair at the Pass—
friends and lovers, the bride beside the bridegroom—
and moved into position to die.
Stranger, take this message to the Spartans:
"We lie here obedient to your laws."

Xerxes and Alexander

Xerxes sailed the slopes of Mount Athos (such
the lies of poets) and paved the sea with ships;
his chariots rolled down a boulevard of decks,
breakfasting Persians drank whole rivers dry—
but tell us how this King of Kings returned
from Salamis in a single ship
scything for searoom through his own drowned. . . .
One world was much too small for Alexander,
double-marching to gain the limits of the globe,
as if he were a runner at Marathon;
early however he reached the final goal,
his fatal Babylon walled with frail dry brick.
A grave was what he wanted. Death alone
shows us what tedious things our bodies are.

Alexander

His sweet moist eye missed nothing—the vague guerilla,
new ground, new tactics, the time for his hell-fire drive,
Demosthenes knotting his nets of dialectic—
phalanxes oiled ten weeks before their trial,
engines on oxen for the fall of Tyre—
Achilles . . . in Aristotle's annotated copy—
health burning like the dewdrop on his flesh
hit in a hundred calculated sallies
to give the Persians the cup of love, of brothers—
the wine-bowl of the Macedonian drinking bout . . .
drinking out of friendship, then meeting Medius,
then drinking, then bathing, then sleeping, then meeting Medius,
then drinking, then bathing . . . dead at thirty-two—
in this life only is our hope in Christ.

Death of Alexander

The young man's numinous eye is like the sun,
for three days the Macedonian soldiers pass;
speechless, he knows them as if they were his sheep.
Shall Alexander be carried in the temple
to pray there, and perhaps, recover? But
the god forbids it, "It's a better thing
if the king stay where he is." He soon dies,
this after all, perhaps, the "better thing." . . .
No one was like him. Terrible were his crimes—
but if you wish to blackguard the Great King,
think how mean, obscure and dull you are,
your labors lowly and your merits less—
we know this, of all the kings of old,
he alone had the greatness of heart to repent.

Poor Alexander, poor Diogenes

Alexander extended philosophy
farther than Aristotle or the honest man,
and kept his foot on everything he touched—
no dog stretching at the Indian sun.
Most dogs find liberty in servitude;
but this is a dog who justified his statue—
Diogenes had his niche in the Roman villas
honored as long as Rome could bear his weight—
cunis, cynic, dog, Diogenes.
Poor Diogenes growling at Alexander,
"You can only do one thing for me, stand out of my sun."
When the schoolboys stole his drinking cup,
he learned to lap up water in his hands—
"No men in Athens . . . only Spartan boys."

The Republic

Didn't Plato ban philosopher-professors,
the idols of the young, from the Republic?
And diehard republicans? It wasn't just
the artist. The Republic! But it never was,
except in the sky-ether of Plato's thought,
steam from the horsedung of his city-state—
Utopia dimmed before the blueprint dried. . . .
America planned one . . . Herman Melville
fixed at that helm, facing a pot of coals,
the sleet and wind spinning him ninety degrees:
"I must not give me up then to the fire,
lest it invert my fire; it blinded me,
so did it me." There's a madness that is woe,
and there is a wisdom that is madness.

Rome

Rome asked for the sun, as much as arms can handle—
liquidation with principle, the proconsul's
rapidity, coherence, and royal *we.* . . .
Thus General Sulla once, again, forever;
and Marius, the people's soldier, was Sulla
doubled, and held the dirt of his low birth
as licence from the gods to thin the rich—
both pulled pistols when they heard foreign tongues,
praised defoliation of the East. . . .
Their faith was lowly, and their taxes high.
The emperor was killed, his métier lived—
Constantine died in office thanks to God.
Whether we buy less or more has long
since fallen to the archeologist's pick.

Hannibal 1. Roman Disaster at the Trebia

The dawn of an ill day whitens the heights.
The camp wakes. Below, the river grumbles and rolls,
and light Numidian horsemen water their horses;
everywhere, sharp clear blasts of the trumpeters.
Though warned by Scipio, and the lying augurs,
the Trebia in flood, the blowing rain,
the Consul Sempronius, proud of his new glory,
has raised the axe for battle, he marches his lictors.
A gloomy flamboyance reddens the dull sky,
Gallic villages smoulder on the horizon.
Far off, the hysterical squeal of an elephant. . . .
Down there, below a bridge, his back on the arch,
Hannibal listens, thoughtful, glorying,
to the dead tramp of the advancing Roman legions.

Hannibal 2. The Life

Throw Hannibal on the scales, how many pounds
does the First Captain come to? This is he
who found the plains of Africa too small,
and Ethiopia's elephants a unique species.
He scaled the Pyrenees, the snow, the Alps—
nature blocked his road, he derricked mountains. . . .
Now Italy is his. "Think nothing is done,
till Rome cracks and my standards fly in the Forum."
What a face for a painter; look, he's a one-eye.
The glory? He's defeated like the rest,
serves some small tyrant farting off drunken meals . . .
and dies by taking poison. . . . Go, Madman, cross
the Alps, the Tiber—be a purple patch
for schoolboys, and their theme for declamation.

Marcus Cato 234–149 B.C.

My live telephone swings crippled to solitude
two feet from my ear; as so often and so often,
I hold your dialogue away to breathe—
still this is love, Old Cato forgoing his wife,
then jumping her in thunderstorms like *Juppiter Tonans*;
his forthrightness gave him long days of solitude,
then deafness changed his gifts for rule to genius.
Cato knew from the Greeks that empire is hurry,
and dominion never goes to the phlegmatic—
it was hard to be Demosthenes in his stone-deaf Senate:
"Carthage must die," he roared . . . and Carthage died.
He knew a blindman looking for gold
in a heap of dust must take the dust with the gold,
Rome, if built at all, must be built in a day.

Marcus Cato 95–42 B.C.

As a boy he was brought to Sulla's villa, The Tombs,
saw people come in as men, and leave as heads.
"Why hasn't someone killed him?" he asked. They answered,
"Men fear Sulla even more than they hate him."
He asked for a sword, and wasn't invited back. . . .
He drowned Plato in wine all night with his friends,
gambled his life in the forum, was stoned like Paul,
and went on talking till soldiers saved the State,
saved Caesar. . . . At the last cast of his lost Republic,
he bloodied his hand on the slave who hid his sword;
he fell in a small sleep, heard the dawn birds chirping,
but couldn't use his hand well . . . when they tried to put
his bowels back, he tore them. . . . He's where he would be:
one Roman who died, perhaps, for Rome.

Horace: Pardon for a Friend

"Under the consulship of Marcus Brutus,
Citizen! We lived out Phillipi, the stampede
when two Republican legions broke like women,
and I threw away my little shield.
Minerva must have helped me to escape;
Pompey, the wave of battle sucked you under,
carried you bleeding in the frantic ebb—
to exile . . . and pardon. What brings you back to Rome,
our glum gods, our hot African sky?
Let us give this banquet to the gods—
do not spare the winejar at your feet.
We'll twist red roses in our myrtle garlands,
it's sweet to drink to fury when my friend is safe—
throw down the dice, and then throw down the dice."

Cicero, the Sacrificial Killing

It's somewhere, somewhere, thought beats stupidly—
a scarlet patch of Tacitus or the Bible,
Pound's Cantos lost in the rockslide of history?
The great man flees his greatness, fugitive husk
of Cicero or Marius without a toga,
old sheep sent out to bite the frosty stubble.
Fascism is too much money for what we are,
a republic keeping, freezing the high ranks,
with heavy feet getting the baby enough milk.
Cicero bold, garrulous in his den
chatting as host on his sofa of magazines;
a squad of state doctors stands by him winking . . .
he minds his hands shaking, and they keep shaking;
if infirmity has a color, it isn't yellow.

44

Ovid and Caesar's Daughter

"I was a modern. In the Emperor's eye,
a tomcat with the number of the Beast—
now buried where Turkey faces the red east,
or wherever Tomi my place of exile was.
Rome asked for art in earnest; at her call
came Lucan, Tacitus and Juvenal,
the black republicans who tore the tits
and bowels of the Mother Wolf to bits. . . .
Thieves pick gold
from the fine print and volume of the Colossus.
Because I loved and wrote too profligately,
Imperial Tiber, O my yellow Wolf,
black earth by the Black Roman Sea, I lie
libelled with the boy-crazy daughter of

Caesar Augustus who will never die."

Antony

"The headache, the night of no performance, duskbreak:
limping home by the fountain's Dionysiac gushes,
water smote from marble, the felon water,
the watery alcoholic going underground
to a stone wife. . . . We were an empire, soul-brothers
to Rome and Alexandria, their imperishable
hope to go beyond the growth of hope.
Am I your only lover who always died?
We were right to die instead of doing nothing,
fearfully backstepping in the dark night of lust.
My hand is shaking, and your breasts are breathing,
white bull's eyes, watchful knobs, in cups of tan
flat on the leather and horn of Jupiter—
daring to raise my privates to the Godhead."

Antony and Cleopatra

Righteous rioters once were revelers,
and had the ear and patronage of kings:
if the king were Antony, he gave
army escorts, and never lost a servant.
At daybreak he fell from heaven to his bed:
next day he handled his winehead like old wine;
yet would notice the fleece of the cirrus, gold, distant,
maidenhair burning heaven's blue nausée,
and knew he lacked all substance: "If I could cure
by the Nile's green slot, a leaf of green papyrus—
I'll taste, God willing, the imperial wine no more,
nor thirst for Cleopatra in my sleep."
"You will drink the Nile to desert," she thinks.
"If God existed, this prayer would prove he didn't."

Cleopatra Topless

"If breast-feeding is servile and for the mammals,
the best breasts in the nightclub are fossils—
a single man couldn't go nearer than the bar;
by listing, I felt the rotations of her breeze;
dancing, she flickered like the family hearth.
She was the old foundation of western marriage. . . .
One was not looking for a work of art—
what do men want? Boobs, bottoms, legs . . . in that order—
the one thing necessary that most husbands
want and yet forgo. She's Cleopatra,
no victim of strict diet, but fulfilment—
chicken turtle climbing up the glass,
managing her invertebrae like hands—
the body of man's crash-love, and her affliction."

46

Nunc est bibendum, Cleopatra's Death

Nunc est bibendum, nunc pede liberum
the time to drink and dance the earth in rhythm.
Before this it was infamous to banquet,
while Cleopatra plotted to enthrone
her depravity naked in the Capitol—
impotent, yet drunk on fortune's favors!
Caesar has tamed your soul, you see with a
now sober eye the scowling truth of terror—
O Cleopatra scarcely escaping with a single ship
Caesar, three decks of oars—O scarcely escaping
when the sparrowhawk falls on the soft-textured dove. . . .
You found a more magnanimous way to die,
not walking on foot in triumphant Caesar's triumph,
no queen now, but a private woman much humbled.

Caligula 1

"I am like the king of a rain-country, rich
though sterile, young but no longer spry enough
to kill vacation in boredom with my dogs—
nothing cheers me, drugs, nieces, falconry,
my triple bed with coral Augustan eagles—
my patrician maids in waiting for whom
all princes are beautiful cannot put on
low enough dresses to heat my skeleton.
The doctor pounding pearls to medicine
finds no formula to cleanse a poisoned vein.
Not even our public happiness sealed with blood,
our tyrant's solace in senility,
great Caesar's painkiller, can strengthen my blood,
green absinthe of forgetfullness, not blood."

Caligula 2

My namesake, Little Boots, Caligula,
tell me why I got your name at school—
Item: your body hairy, badly made,
head hairless, smoother than your marble head;
Item: eyes hollow, hollow temples, red
cheeks roughed with blood, legs spindly, hands that leave
a clammy snail's trail on your scarlet sleeve,
your hand no hand could hold . . . bald head, thin neck—
you wished the Romans had a single neck.
That was no artist's sadism. Animals
ripened for your arenas suffered less
than you when slaughtered—yours the lawlessness
of something simple that has lost its law,
my namesake, not the last Caligula.

Empress Messalina's last Bridegroom

Tell me what advice you have to give
the fellow Caesar's consort wants to marry—
the last man, the most beautiful an old
patrician family has to offer . . . soon turned
from life to death by Messalina's eye.
She has long been seated, her bridal veil
is purple, her lover's bed of imperial roses
rustles invitingly, quite openly, in the garden—
now by ancient rule, her dowery of a million
sesterces is counted out—signatories,
lawyers, the green-lipped diviner, attend on tiptoe. . . .
"Say no, you'll die before the lamps are lit.
Say yes, you'll live till the city hears . . . her husband,
the Emperor Claudius last in Rome to know."

48

Weekly Juvenal, Late-Empire

In the days of Saturn, so he wrote,
Chastity still lingered on the earth—
a good son, soft-textured, eyes in the back of his head,
with a snobbish tassel on his plunger,
his apocalyptic disappointments
sobbing thunder for his melting caste—
poets' jamble-jangle to make confused thought deep . . .
Roma Meretrix, in your sick day
only women had the hearts of men.
Marx, a Juvenal in apotheosis, thought
the poor were Saturnians shaking us from below—
his romantic alchemy. He had no answer—
tomorrow-yesterday the world was young,
and parents had no children of their own.

Juvenal's Prayer

What's best, what serves us . . . leave it to the gods.
We're dearer to the gods than to ourselves.
Harassed by impulse and diseased desire,
we ask for wives, and children by those wives—
what wives and children heaven only knows.
Still if you will ask for something, pray for
a healthy body and a healthy soul,
a mind that is not terrified of death,
thinks length of days the least of nature's gifts—
courage that drives out anger and longing . . . our hero,
Hercules, and the pain of his great labor. . . .
Success is worshipped as a god; it's we
who set her up in palace and cathedral.
I give you simply what you have already.

Vita Brevis

The whistling arrow flies less eagerly,
and bites the bullseye less ferociously;
the Roman chariot grinds the docile sand
of the arena less violently to round the post. . . .
How silently, how hurriedly, we run
through life to die. You doubt this, animal
blinded by the light? Each ascending sun
dives like a cooling meteorite to its fall,
Licio. Did dead Carthage affirm what you deny?
Death only throws fixed dice, yet you will raise
the ante, and stake your life on every toss.
Those hours will hardly pardon us their loss,
those brilliant hours that wore away our days,
our days that ate into eternity.

The Good Life

To see their trees flower and leaves pearl with mist,
fan out above them on the wineglass elms,
life's frills and the meat of life: wife, children, houses;
decomposition burning out in service—
or ass-licking for medals on Caesar's peacock lawn,
tossing birdseed to enslaved aristocrats,
vomiting purple in the vapid baths.
Crack legions and new religions hold the Eagle—
Rome of the officers, dull, martyred, anxious to please.
Men might ask how her imperial machine,
never pleasant and a hail of gallstone,
keeps beating down its Caesars raised for murder,
though otherwise forgotten . . . pearls in the spiked necklace—
the price of slavery is ceaseless vigilance.

Rome in the Sixteenth Century

You come to Rome to look for Rome, O Pilgrim!
in Christian Rome there is no room for Rome,
the Aventine is its own mound and tomb;
her Capitol that crowned the forum rubble,
a laid out corpse her smart brick walls she boasted of;
her medals filed down by the hand of time
say more was lost to chance and time
than Hannibal or Caesar could consume.
Only the Tiber has remained, a small
shallow current which used to wash a city,
and now bewails her sepulcher. O Rome!
from all your senates, palms, dominions, bronze
and beauty, what was firm has fled. Whatever
was fugitive maintains its permanence.

Attila, Hitler

Hitler had fingertips of apprehension,
"Who knows how long I'll live? Let us have war.
We *are* the barbarians, the world is near the end."
Attila mounted on raw meat and greens
galloped to massacre in his single fieldmouse suit,
he never left a house that wasn't burning,
could only sleep on horseback, sinking deep
in his rural dream. Would he have found himself
in this coarsest, cruelest, least magnanimous,
most systematic, most philosophical . . .
a nomad stay-at-home: *He who has, has*;
a barbarian wondering why the old world collapsed,
who also left his festering fume of refuse,
old tins, dead vermin, ashes, eggshells, youth?

Mohammed

Like Henry VIII, Mohammed got religion
in the dangerous years, and smashed the celibates,
haters of life, though never takers of it—
changed their monasteries to foundries,
reset their non-activist Buddhistic rote
to the *schrecklichkeit* and warsongs of his tribe.
The Pope still twangs his harp for chastity—
the boys of the jihad on a string of unwitting camels
rush paradise, halls stocked with adolescent
beauties, both sexes for simple nomad tastes—
how warmly they sleep in tile-abstraction alcoves;
love is resurrection, and her war a rose:
woman wants man, man woman, as naturally
as the thirsty frog desires the rain.

Fame

We bleed for people, so independent and selfsuspecting,
if the door is locked, they come back tomorrow, instead of
      knocking—
hearts scarred by complaints they would not breathe;
it was not their good fortune to meet their love;
however long they lived, they would still be waiting.
They knew princes show kindness by humiliation. . . .
Timur said something like: "The drop of water
that fails to become a river is food for the dust.
The eye that cannot size up the Bosphorus
in a single drop is an acorn, not the eye of a man. . . ."
Timur's face was like the sun on a dewdrop;
the path to death was always under his foot—
this the sum of the world's scattered elements,
fame, a bouquet in the niche of forgetfulness.

Timur Old

To wake some midnight, on that instant senile,
clasping clay knees . . . in this unwarlike posture
meet your grandsons, a sheeted, shivering mound,
pressed racecar hideously scared, agog with headlight—
Timur . . . his pyramid half a million heads,
one skull and then one brick and then one skull,
live art that makes the Arc de Triomphe pale.
Even a modernist must be new at times,
not a parasite on his own tradition,
its too healthy sleep that foreshadows death.
A thing well done, even a pile of heads
modestly planned to wilt before the builder,
is art, if art is anything won from nature. . . .
We weep for the sword as much as for the victims—

fealty affirmed when friendship was a myth.

Northmen

These people were provincials with the wind
behind them, and a gently swelling birthrate,
scattering galleys and their thin crews
of pirates from Greenland to the lung of the Thames. . . .
The Skyfleets hover coolly in mirage;
our bombers are clean-edged as Viking craft,
to pin the Third World to its burning house. . . .
Charlemagne loved his three R's, and feared the future
when he saw the first Northmen row out on the Rhine:
we are begotten in sorrow to die in joy—
their humor wasn't brevity but too few words,
ravishment trailing off in the midnight sun,
illumination, then bewilderment,
the glitter of the Viking in the icecap.

End of the Saga

"Even if they murder the whole world,
we'll hit them so hard, they'll never tell the story."
Kriemhild was shouting, "If they get to the air,
and cool their coats of mail, we will be lost."
When the great hall was fired, we saw them kneel
beside their corpses, and drink the flowing blood—
unaccustomed to such drink, they thought it good,
in the great heat, it tasted cooler than wine.
They tried to lift their brothers from the fire,
they found them too hot to hold, and let them drop.
"O why are we so wet with our lifeblood?
Beines brichts, herzen nichts. . . ."
Kriemhild on horseback laughs at them, as well she may,
the house is burned, and all her enemies killed.

Death of Count Roland

King Marsiliun of Saragossa
does not love God, he is carried to the shade of the orchard,
and sits reclining on his bench of blue tile,
with more than twenty thousand men about him;
his speech is only the one all kings must make,
it did not spark the Franco-Moorish War. . . .
At war's-end Roland's brains seeped from his ears;
he called for the Angel Michael, his ivory horn,
prayed for his peers, and scythed his sword, Durendal—
farther away than a man might shoot a crossbow,
toward Saragossa, there is a grassy place,
Roland went to it, climbed the little mound:
a beautiful tree there, four great stones of marble—
on the green grass, he has fallen back, has fainted.

Eloise and Abelard

We know what orthodox analysis
could do with her, the talented, the taloned
cat hooked on the cold fish of Abelard.
They were one soul, but now her mind is dust,
and his assaulted ember is extinct.
After his imprisonment, energy came
to the woman such as she had never known,
sprinkling Paris like a fresh flow of blood,
old Sorbonne argot, shit on Saint Bernard
in love with his voice and sold to the police. . . .
Abelard's tortured debater's points
once flew to the mark, feathered with her ecstasy,
and stamping students, then he fell like lightning,
in love with *the dialectic*, his Minerva.

Joinville and Louis IX

"Given my pilgrim's scarf and staff, I left
the village of Joinville on foot, barefoot, in my shirt,
never turning my eyes for fear my heart would melt
at leaving my mortgaged castle, my two fair children—
a Crusader? Some of us were, and lived to be ransomed.
Bishops, nobles, and Brothers of the King
strolled free in Acre, and begged the King to sail home,
and leave the meaner folk. Sore of heart then,
I went to a barred window, and passed my arms through the bars
of the window, and someone came, and leant on my shoulders,
and placed his two hands on my forehead—Philip de Nemours?
I screamed, 'Leave me in peace!' His hand dropped by chance,
and I knew the King by the emerald on his finger:
'If I should leave Jerusalem, who will remain?'"

55

The Army of the Duc de Nemours

Yeats anxiously warned us not to lend a high
degree of reality to the Great War.
There are wars and wars, and some are high-notes
on the scale of sexual delirium
running the gamut of Moses' anathemas:
wantonness, sodomy, bestiality.
I am a Catholic because I am a wanton.
Italian mercenaries besieging Lyons
for the Duc de Nemours huzzaed great flocks
of goats before them—no billies, two thousand udders
decked out in green sportcoats fringed with gold.
They served a sound man for a mistress. Small war,
one far distant from our army mascots—
but who will tell us now what Lyons paid?

Dante 1

In his dark day, Dante made the mistake of treating
politicians as if they belonged to life,
not ideology. In his Vision
his poor souls eclipse the black and white of God.
A man running for his life will never tire:
his Ser Brunetto ran through hell like one
who ran for the green cloth through the green fields
at Verona, looking more like one
who won the roll of cloth, than those who lost. . . .
All comes from a girl met at the wrong time,
losing her color as she fared and brightened;
God and her love called Dante forth to exile
in midwintertime cold and lengthening days,
when the brief field frost mimics her sister, snow.

Dante 2

Torn darlings and professional sparring partners,
will we ever grow wiser or kinder in
the exercise of marriage—its death
like this summer landscape chilling under
the first influence of the evening star
winking from green to black—our bodies, black
before we even know that we are dead.
Dante loved Beatrice beyond her life,
with a loyalty outside anywhere;
all icy pandemonium . . . a girl
too early his enchanter and too late,
the hour half-over when every star was shining—
lightning piercing his marriage's slow fire,
some brightest prong, antennae of an ant.

Dante 3. Buonconte

"No one prays for me . . . Giovanna or the others."
What took you so far from Campaldino
we never found your body? "Where the Archiano
at the base of the Casentino loses its name
and becomes the Arno, I stopped running,
the war lost, and wounded in the throat—
flying on foot and splashing the field with blood.
There I lost sight and speech, and died saying *Maria*. . . .
I'll tell you the truth, tell it to the living,
an angel and devil fought with claws for my soul:
You angel, why do you rob me for his last word?
The rain fell, then the hail, my body froze,
until the raging Archiano snatched me,
and loosened my arms I'd folded like the cross."

Dante 4. Paolo and Francesca

And she to me, "What sorrow is greater to us
than returning from misery to the sweet time?
If you will know the first root of our love,
I'll speak as one who must both speak and weep.
On that day we were reading for dalliance
of Lancelot, and how love brought him down;
we were alone there and without suspicion,
often something we read made our eyes meet—
we lost color. A single moment destroyed us: reading
how her loved smile was kissed by such a lover.
He who never will be divided from me
came to me trembling, and kissed my shaking mouth.
That book and he who wrote it was a bawd,
a Galahalt. That day we read no further."

Dante 5. Wind

The night blowing through the world's hospital is human,
Francesca's strife and monotony blown
by the folly of Christendom that loathed her flesh—
seed winds, the youthful breath of the old world,
each a progression of our carnal pleasure
and a firm extension of the soul. . . .
The girl has been rowing her boat since early morning,
hard riding has never blistered her agile thighs.
The snail, a dewdrop, stumbles like the blind,
puts out his little horns to feel the sun.
In the garden of Allah, man still wears the beard,
the women are undressed, accepting love. . . .
They loved if one or two days of life meant much,
then an eternity of failed desire—

winds fed the fire, a wind can blow it out.

Canterbury

Regret those jousting aristocracies,
war-bright, though sportsmen, life a round of games;
sex horsed their chivalry, even when
the aggressor was only an artless dragon. . . .
The Black Prince clamps a missal in his hands,
rests, stone-chainmail, *imprimatur*, on his slab;
behind the spasms of his ruffian hand,
slept a public school and pious faith in murder—
gallantry sobered by suppression.
At Canterbury a guilty pilgrim may ask:
"Have I the right to my imagination?"
Here the great fighter Captain lies with those
who made it, those whom fate disdained to wound.
All's masonry . . . theirs the new day, as the old.

Coleridge and Richard II

Coleridge wasn't flatter-blinded by
his kinship with Richard II . . . a *feminine friendism*,
the constant overflow of imagination
proportioned to his dwindling will to act.
Richard unkinged saw shipwreck in the mirror,
not the King; womanlike, he feared
he must see himself more frequently to exist,
the white glittering inertia of the iceberg.
Coleridge had the cheering fancy only blacks
would cherish slavery for two thousand years;
though most negroes in 1800 London were
onwardlooking and by culture further
from gilding jungles and dead kings than Coleridge,
the one poet who blamed his failure on himself.

Dames du Temps jadis

Say in what country, where
is Flora, the Roman,
Archipaida or Thais
far lovelier,
or Echo whose voice would answer
across the land or river—
her beauty more than human.
Where is our wise Eloise
and Peter Abelard
gelded at Saint Denis
for love of her—
Jehanne the good maid of Lorraine
the English burned at Rouen?
Where, mother of God, is last year's snow?

Bosworth Field

In a minute, two inches of rain stream through my dry
garden stones, clear as crystal, without trout—
we have gone down and down, gone the wrong brook
Robespiërre and Stalin mostly killed people they knew,
Richard the Third was Dickon, Duke of Gloucester,
long arm of the realm, goddam blood royal,
terrible underpinning of what he let breathe.
No wonder, we have dug him up past proof,
still fighting drunk on mortal wounds,
ready to gallop down his own apologist.
What does he care for Thomas More and Shakespeare
pointing fingers at his polio'd body;
for the moment, he is king; he is the king
saying: *it's better to have lived, than live.*

Cow

The moon is muffled behind a ledge of cloud,
briefly douses its bonfire on the harbor. . . .
Machiavelli despised those spuriously fought
Italian mounted-mercenary battles;
Corinthian tactics, Greek met Greek; one death,
he died of a stroke, but not the stroke of battle.
The Italians were not diehards even for peace—
our police hit more to terrorize than kill;
clubs break and minds, women hosed down stairs—
am I crippled for life? . . . A cow has guts,
screwed, she lives for it as much as we,
a three-day mother, then a working mother;
the calf goes to the calfpool. . . . When their barn has been burned,
cows will look into the sunset and tremble.

Sir Thomas More

Holbein's More, my patron saint as a convert,
the gold chain of S's, the golden rose,
the plush cap, the brow's damp feathertips of hair,
the good eyes' stern, facetious twinkle, ready
to turn from executioner to martyr—
or saunter with the great King's bluff arm on your neck,
feeling that friend-slaying, terror-dazzled heart
baloooning off into its awful dream—
a noble saying, "How the King must love you!"
And you, "If it were a question of my head,
or losing his meanest village in France. . . ."
then by the scaffold and the headsman's axe—
"Friend, give me your hand for the first step,
as for coming down, I'll shift for myself."

Anne Boleyn

The cows of Potter and Albert Cuyp are timeless;
in the depths of Europe, scrawly pastures
and scrawlier hamlets unwatered by paint or Hegel,
the cow is king. None of our rear-guard painters,
lovers of nature and haters of abstraction,
make an art of farming. With a bull's moist eye,
dewlap and misty phallus, Cuyp caught the farthest glisten,
tonnage and rumination of the sod. . . .
There was a whiteness to Anne Boleyn's throat,
shiver of heresy, *raison d'état*,
the windfall abandon of a Giorgione,
Renaissance high hand with nature—only the lovely,
the good, the wealthy serve the Venetian, whose art
knows nothing yet of husbandry and cattle.

Death of Anne Boleyn

Summer hail flings crystals on the window—
they wrapped the Lady Anne's head in a white handkerchief. . . .
To Wolsey, *the nightcrow*, but to Anthony Froude,
stoic virtue spoke from her stubborn lips and chin—
five adulteries in three years of marriage;
the game was hotly charged. "I hear say I'll
not die till noon; I am very sorry therefore,
I thought to be dead this hour and past my pain."
Her jailor told her that beheading is painless—
"It is subtle." "I have a little neck,"
she said, and put her hands about it laughing.
Her Husband hoped she'd have small displeasure in her death—
no foreigners, though by the King's abundance
the scene was open to any Englishman.

Cranach's Man-Hunt

Composed, you will say, for our forever friendship,
almost one arm around our many shoulders,
a cloud darkens the stream of the photograph,
friends bound by birth and faith . . . one German outing.
We are game for the deer-hunt, aged five to ninety,
seniority no key to who will die
on this clearing of blown, coarse grass, a trap in the landscape,
a green bow in the bend of a choppy, lavender stream,
eighteen or nineteen of us, bounding, swimming—
stags and does . . . the Kaiser Maximilian
and the wise Saxon Elector, screened by one clump,
winch their crossbows . . . the horsemen, picadors,
whipped to action by their beautiful, verminous dogs . . .
this battle the Prince has never renounced or lost.

Charles V by Titian

But we cannot go back to Charles V
barreled in armor, more gold fleece than king;
he haws on the gristle of a Flemish word,
his upper and lower Hapsburg jaws won't meet.
The sunset he tilts at is big Venetian stuff,
the true Charles, done by Titian, never lived.
The battle he rides offstage to is offstage.
No St. Francis, he did what Francis shied at,
gave up office, one of twenty monarchs
since Saturn who willingly made the grand refusal.
In his burgherish monastery, he learned he couldn't
put together a clock with missing parts.
He had dreamed of a democracy of Europe,
and carried enemies with him in a cage.

Execution 1

(FROM CHIDIOCK TICHBORNE 1568-86)

"I saw the world, and yet I was not seen;
fear comes more often now, and no less sharp
than in the year of my first razor and the death of God.
My tongue thickened as if anesthetized,
and I saw a painted fish blow live bubbles,
the wallpaper flowers drank plaster, turned to moss. . . .
The anachronistic axe sighs in its block;
a little further on, I will be nature,
my head a speck of white salt on a white plate,
lying on call forever, never called. . . .
At the Resurrection, will I start awake,
and find my head upon my shoulders again
singing the dawnless alba of the gerontoi?
Old age is all right, but it has no future.

Execution 2

"Asleep just now, just now I am awake—
my face the jack of hearts on a playing card;
my trousers are too bleached green; my coat wet leaf;
my fair young flesh sky-green of my sad vein.
I turn the card, and I am trees or grass—
last summer for the wondering mind, for seeing
the good servant's green grave outside the pale . . .
veined marble mantel, rolled rug, the sheeted den,
the old master covered with his pillowslip—
I searching as everyman for my one good deed,
crying love lost in my short apprenticeship,
regretting my long-vanished art of breathing,
knowing I must forget how to breathe through my mouth:
now I am dead, and just now I was made."

Marlowe

Vain surety of man's mind so near to death,
twenty-nine years with hopes to total fifty—
one blurred, hurried, still undecoded month
hurled Marlowe from England to his companion shades.
His mighty line denies his shady murder:
"How uncontrollably sweet and swift my life
with two London hits and riding my high tide,
drinking out May in Deptford with three friends,
one or all four perhaps in Secret Service.
Christ was a bastard, His Testament's filthily Greeked—
I died swearing, stabbed with friends who knew me—
was it the bar-check? . . . Tragedy is to die . . .
for that vacant parsonage, Posterity;
my plays are stamped in bronze, my life in tabloid."

Duc de Guise

The grip gets puffy, and water wears the stones—
O to be always young among our friends,
as one of the countless peers who graced the world
with their murders and *joie de vivre*, made good
in a hundred aimless amorous bondages. . . .
The irregular hero, Henri, Duc de Guise,
Pope and Achilles of the Catholic League,
whose canopy and cell I saw at Blois—
just before he died, at the moment of orgasm,
his round eyes, hysterical and wistful,
a drugged bull breathing, a cool, well-pastured brain,
the muscular slack of his stomach swelling
as if he were pregnant . . . his small sword unable
to encircle the circle of his killers.

Mary Stuart

"We ran for our lives on the nightslope, gained the car,
my maxi-coat, Tsar officer's, dragged the snow,
you and I killed my husband, and stained the snow.
Romance of the snowflakes! Men swarm up the night,
grass pike in overalls with scythe and pitchfork;
shouting, 'Take the car, we'll smash the girl. . . .'
Once queens were on firstname terms with the poor,
a car was a castle, and inheritance stuck to the rich. . . .
We roared off hell-wheel and scattered the soft mob;
happily only one man splashed the windshield,
we dared not pluck him off; it was hard at night
to hold the road with a carcass on the windshield. . . ."
At nightmare-end, the bedroom, the dark night of marriage,
the bloodiest hands joined, and took no more blood.

The Wife of Henri Quatre 1

"O cozy scuffles, soft obscenities,
wardrobes that dragged the exchequer to its knees,
cables of pearl and crazy lutes strung tight—
tension, groin and backbone! Every night
I kicked our pillows and embroidered lies
to famish the King's purse. I said his eyes
flew kiting to my dormer from the blue.
I was a sparrow. He was fifty-two. . . .
Alas, my brutal girlish moodswings drove
my Husband, wrenched and giddy, from the Louvre,
to sleep in single lodgings on the town. . . .
He feared the fate of kings who died in sport;
murder cut him short—
a kitchen-knife honed on a carriage-wheel."

The Wife of Henri Quatre 2

"I show no emotion, king must follow king;
the seasons circle, fall to laughing rings
of scything children. I rock my nightmare son,
I see his dimpled fingers clutch Versailles,
take ball and scepter; he asks the Queen to die.
And so I press a lover's palm to mine,
I am his vintage and his living vine,
oozing, entangling . . . a moment, a moment, a moment—
even a queen must divert her precious time.
Henri Quatre—how you used to look
for blood and pastime! If you ever loved
in this Kingdom where you let your scepter drop,
pardon the easy virtues of the earth. . . .
Your great nerve gone, Sire, sleep without a care."

Malesherbes, l'Homme de Lettres

The duplicitous opportunism of
the unreconstructable master of plain French—
giving Horatian balance to your vengeance . . .
fierce and measuring with the best almost,
a winner by tying rivals in the ropes,
verse your chisel to make France a classic.
You took your disciples' measure, and kept them apart,
small enough to sing on the crown of your hat—
lay priest, a friend with bantam gaiety
neither wine or abstraction could corrupt—
your last profession of letters is writing letters,
writing a strayed friend's relenting wife:
"For an atheist Calvinist, you show
depths of compassion reserved the Virgin Mary."

Góngora, the Tomb of Cardinal Sandoval

This chapel that you gaze at, these stern tombs,
the pride of architecture . . . Ah traveller,
diamonds were blunted on this porphyry,
the teeth of files wore smooth as ice—this vault
seals up the dust of one who never let
the earth oppress him. Whose? If you would know,
stay and study this inscription. Words
give marble meaning and a voice to bronze.
Generous devotion binds this urn
with majesty and with propriety
to the heroic ashes of Sandoval,
who left his coat of arms, once five blue stars
on a gold field, to climb with surer step
through the blue sky, and scale the golden stars.

Spain Lost

Miré los muros de la patria mía
I saw the musty shingles of my house,
raw wood in place once, now a wash of moss
eroded by the ruin of the age
turning all fair and green things into waste.
I climbed the pasture. I saw the dim sun drink
the ice just thawing from the bouldered fallow,
scrub crowd the orchard, seize the summer's yield,
and higher up, the sickly cattle bellow.
I went into my house. I saw how dust
and ravel had devoured its furnishing;
even my stick was withered and more bent,
even my sword was coffined up in rust—
there was no hilt left for my hand to try.
Everything ached, and told me I must die.

68

Rembrandt

His faces crack . . . if mine could crack and breathe!
His Jewish Bridegroom, hand spread on the Jewish Bride's
bashful, tapestried, level bosom, is faithful;
a girl, half-shadow, gives soul to his flayed steer.
Her breasts, the snowdrops, have lasted out the storm.
The Dutchman was a sack, his woman a sack,
the obstinate, undefeated hull of an old scow;
but Bathsheba's ample stomach, her heavy, practical feet,
are reverently dried by the faithful servant,
his eyes dwell lovingly on each fulfilled sag;
her unfortunate body is the privilege of service,
is radiant with an homage void of possession. . . .
We see, if we see at all, through a brown mist
the strange new idol for the marketplace.

Milton in Separation

His wife was no loss to the cool and Christian Homer,
blind, paraphrasing Latin and pronouncing
divorce and *marriage* with hard, sardonic R's.
Through the blank strain of separation, he learned
he only cared for life in the straits. Her flight
put a live elbow in his marble Eve;
she filled a thirst for emptiness—
when she struck, he fell hookloose from her fireflesh,
free to serve what wooed him most, his writing,
the overobsession posterity must pay
on the great day when the eyelids of life lift,
and blind eyes shiver in the draft of heaven,
and goldfinch flame in the tinderbush—
to set the woods on fire and warm the glacier.

69

Marriage

Once the stoneaxe surrendered its Celt soul,
civilized marriage allowed a day for give-out,
four legs at Bible meeting on the loveseat. . . .
From the womb, I say, I scorned Leviathan,
found my intemperate, apocalyptic terms,
host to ten thousand ethnic sovereignties stuck
with strange tongues; the Garden open to all and free. . . .
Too long we've hungered for its ancient fruit,
marriage with its naked artifice;
two practised animals, and close to widow
and widower, greedily bending forward
for a last handgrasp of vermillion leaves,
clinging like bloodclots to the smitten branch—
fibrous growths . . . green, sweet, golden, black.

Samuel Pepys

A modern, except for double Sunday prayers,
Samuel Pepys knew what made the Navy float,
how to measure the baulks of timber, test hemp
for fray, what cloth could fly the English flag,
what made his wife fray, her butter-fingers with money,
on sufferance with her servants, her screwy periods
timed with her crushes on the Church of Rome.
Pepys was a religious stroller like Charles II,
old music, with no swerving for transcendence.
"Chance without merit brought me in, only work . . ."
He kept a sensual man's respect for sin.
By tears and prayers he cured himself of drink,
but not of glutting a woman with a look—
an inconsequential, not Hermetic, mind.

70

John Graham at Killicrankie

"The Scotch Lords had the means to salmon fish,
the painter skill to paint them killing salmon,
sunrise or sunset, gray crag and brawling tarn,
poachers stripped, gashed, parceled to the birds . . . .
If we do not fight, we had better break up and die.
In the Highlands, wherever war is not a science,
we humbly ask for nerve in our commander.
Ours kicked off the one pair of shoes in the clan
to march us barefoot. The British drank the grass;
torrents of their redcoats and tartans raving down
the valley to the gorge of Killicrankie. . . .
He waved his sword and opened a gap in his breastplate;
he won the battle, lost his life and Scotland.
If it's well with the King, it matters little to me."

Versailles

Smoke weakens the brilliant summer of Versailles;
marijuana fires fume in the King's back yard.
He breathes the green dust of the end of life,
as though he were in heaven—the peacock spins,
the revolution hasn't evolved to the King,
his cubist garden is square and cone and ball,
no imperfection to aid imagination.
Heaven might be this simple if we could go there,
and see the Sun-King spit into the wind of Versailles;
he cannot tell his left hand from his right,
he holds up two smooth stones, marked *left* and *right*. . . .
In the Hall of Mirrors, the heavy curtains lift,
a head higher, two heads, than the old shrunk dying King—
and dance spontaneously in the atheist air.

Peter the Great in France

"He saw us and Paris with open eyes—
no gloves, gold buttons, a brown coat mostly unbuttoned,
his frequent mouth-convulsions frightful to watch . . .
his hat on the table, never on his head,
even outdoors . . . an air of greatness
natural to him could not be mistaken.
What he drank was inconceivable: at meals,
a quart of brandy, two beers, two bottles of wine—
at Fontainebleau he nearly lost his horse.
For side he had a French interpreter,
though he spoke English and Latin like a consul. . . .
Peter, presented to the child Louis Quinze,
hoisted him up to his eye-level, and smiled—
the superiority of age was felt."

Bishop Berkeley

The Bishop's solipsism is clerical,
no one was much imperiled by his life,
except he sailed to New England and was Irish,
he wasn't an Attila or Rimbaud
driven to unhook his skull to crack the world.
He lived with quality, and thought the world
was only perceptions that he could perceive. . . .
In Mexico, I too caused my private earthquake,
and made the earth tremble in the soles of my feet;
a local insurrection of my blood,
its river system saying: I am I,
I am Whitman, I am Berkeley, all men—
calming my feet in a tub of lukewarm water;
the water that scalded one foot froze the other.

The Worst Sinner, Jonathan Edwards' God

The earliest sportsman in the earliest dawn,
waking to what redness, waking a killer,
saw the red cane was sweet in his red grip;
the blood of the shepherd matched the blood of the wolf.
But Jonathan Edwards prayed to think himself
worse than any man that ever breathed;
he was a good man, and he prayed with reason—
which of us hasn't thought his same thought worse?
Each night I lie me down to heal in sleep;
two or three mornings a week, I wake to my sin—
sins, not sin; not two or three mornings, seven.
God himself cannot wake five years younger,
and drink away the venom in the chalice—
the best man in the best world possible.

Watchmaker God

Say life is the one-way trip, the one-way flight,
say this without hysterical undertones—
then you could say you stood in the cold light of science,
seeing as you are seen, espoused to fact.
 Strange, life is both the fire and fuel; and we,
the animals and objects, must be here
without striking a spark of evidence
that anything that ever stopped living
ever falls back to living when life stops.
There's a pale romance to the watchmaker God
of Descartes and Paley; He drafted and installed
us in the Apparatus. He loved to tinker;
but having perfected what He had to do,
stood off shrouded in his loneliness.

73

Christians

When I am oldfashioned, I hear words,
inner things in us the Lord God alone sees. . . .
David and Bathsheba will never tell me
I step on a thumbtack each time I go to a woman,
if Faith ceases to be a torture-machine, it stops—
I miss the white militia, the subtle schoolmen's
abstract-expressionist idea of salvation:
the haven of their heaven sure and uniform,
rest for the weary and sight for the blind.
Yet we were no kinder when we had the Faith,
and thought the massacred could be reformed,
and move like ironsides through the unwithering white,
squadron on squadron, stiff and sharp and pure—
they move in a body if they move at all.

Dies Irae

On this day of anger, when I am Satan's,
forfeited to that childless sybarite—
Our God, he walks with me, he talks with me,
in sleep, in thunder, and in wind and weather;
he strips the wind and gravel from my words,
and speeds me naked on the single way. . . .
You who save those you must save free; you, whose
least anger makes my faith derelict,
you came from nothing to the earth for me,
my enemies are many, my friends few—
how often do you find me, God, and die?
Once our Lord looked and saw the world was good—
in His hand, God has got us in His hand;
everything points to non-existence except existence.

Pompadour's Daughter

"Our family reunions in what new foreign bar?
Which lover will one's mother service this week?
Her shipowners, generals, peers were bel Antonios,
almost by definition jerks, *les vieux,*
bantering insolence stuffed in wet footballs—
charging on her they did not cheer or shout; they growled. . . .
When I sought fame in Paris, I little knew
how near the fall was: speeches, lecture halls,
vast wombs of echoes bound by injured nerve.
I hoped I'd stay a woman if I only loved
one or two friends. I found a million friends. . . .
Now I want to marry the least man,
the top of whose husbandry is breeding flowers—
no sense in shouting truth from the wrong window."

Life and Civilization

Your skirt stopped half a foot above your knee,
diamonded your birthmarks by your black mesh tights;
and yet I see your legs as perfect legs—
who would want to finger or approach
the rumination in your figured sweater?
Civilization will always outdo life,
if toleration means to bear and hurt—
that's Locke, Voltaire; the Liberal dies for that,
bites his own lip to warm his icy tooth,
and faces all vicissitudes with calmness.
That's why there are none, that's why we're none,
why, unenlightened, we shiver once a moon
whenever Eros arcs into the Virgin—
as you, no virgin, made me bear myself.

Robespierre and Mozart as Stage

Robespierre could live with himself: "The republic
of Virtue without *la terreur* is a disaster.
Loot the chateaux, dole bread to Saint Antoine."
He found the guillotine was not an idler
hearing *mort à Robespierre* from the Convention floor,
the high harsh laughter of the innocents,
the Revolution returning to grand tragedy—
to life the place where we find happiness,
or not at all. . . . Ask the voyeur
what blue movie is worth a look through the keyhole. . . .
Even the prompted Louis Seize was living theater,
sternly and lovingly judged by his critics, who knew
Mozart's barber *Figaro* could never
cut the gold thread of the suffocating curtain.

Saint-Just 1767–93

Saint-Just: his name seems stolen from the Missal. . . .
His chamois coat, the dandy's vast cravate
knotted with pretentious negligence;
he carried his head like the Holy Sacrament.
He thought only the laconic fit to rule
the austerity of his hideous cardboard Sparta.
"I must move with the stone footstep of the sun—
faction plagues the course of revolution,
as reptiles follow the dry bed of a torrent.
I am young and therefore close to nature.
Happiness is a new idea in Europe;
we bronzed liberty with the guillotine.
I'm still twenty, I've done badly, I'll do better."
He did, the scaffold, "Je sais où je vais."

Vision

Sloping, torn black tarpaper on a wet roof,
on several; here and there, an uprooted nail,
a downpour soaking the wooden gingerbread,
old ornamentation too labored for revival,
and too much for its time. My judge was there,
frizzled, powdered to perfection, sky-blue
Robespierre, or anyone's nameless, mercantile
American forefather of 1790—
his head bowed, a hand spiked on each sharp knee—
the cleansing guillotine peeps over his shoulder.
I climb the scaffold, knowing my last words
need not be audible or much to the point,
if my blood will blot my blackest mark—
what does having my life behind me mean?

Napoleon

Our used bookshops, anachronisms from London, are gone
from Boston; hard to guess now why I spent
whole vacations lugging home his hundred *Lives*—
clapping the dust from that stationery stock:
cheap deluxe lithographs and gilt-edged pulp—
a man . . . not bloodthirsty, not sparing of blood,
with an eye and *sang-froid* to manage everything;
his iron hand no mere appendage . . . his solicitude
for improbable contingencies . . .
struck uprooting races, lineage, Jacobins—
the price was paltry . . . three million soldiers dead,
grand opera fixed like morphine in their veins.
Dare we say, he had no moral center?
All gone like the smoke of his own artillery?

Before Waterloo, the Last Night

And night and muffled creakings and the wheels
of the artillery-wagons circling with the clock,
Blucher's Prussian army passing the estate. . . .
The man plays the harpsichord, and lifts his eyes,
playing each air by ear to look at her—
he might be looking in a mirror for himself,
a mirror filled with his young face, the sorrow
his music made seductive and beautiful.
Suddenly everything is over. Instead,
wearily by an open window, she stands
and clasps the helpless thumping of her heart.
No sound. Outside, a fresh morning wind has risen,
and strangely foreign on the mirror-table,
leans his black shako with its white deathshead.

Waterloo

A thundercloud hung on the mantel of our summer
cottage by the owners, Miss Barnard and Mrs Curtis
a sad picture, 2/3's life-scale, removed now, and no doubt
scrapped as too raw and empire for our taste:
Waterloo, Waterloo! You could choose sides then:
the engraving made the blue French uniforms black,
the British Redcoats gray; those running were French—
an aide-de-camp, Napoleon's perhaps,
wore a cascade of overstated braid,
there sabered, dying, his standard wrenched from weak hands;
his killer, a helmeted, fog-gray dragoon—
six centuries, this field of their encounter,
kill-round of French sex against the English *no* . . .
La Gloire fading to *sauve qui peut* and *merde.*

Leaving Home, Marshal Ney

Loved person, I'm never in the clear with conscience,
I hang by a kitetail. Old lovers used to stop
for the village's unreliable clock and bells;
their progress . . . more government, civil service,
the Prussian school, the Irish constable,
hardware exploding help on the city poor.
The *Ancien Régime* locked in place at the tap of a glove;
those long steel scoopnets lie rolled in the bureau. . . .
I hear the young voice of a fresher age and habit,
walking to fame or Paris: "You little knew
I could hardly put one foot before the other.
I passed through many varieties of untried being,
a Marshal of France, and shot for too much courage—
why should shark be eaten when bait swim free?"

Beethoven

Our cookbook is bound like Whitman's *Leaves of Grass*—
gold title on green. I have escaped its death,
take two eggs with butter, drink and smoke;
I live past possibility, not prudence—
who can banquet on the shifting cloud,
lie to friends and tell the truth in print,
be Othello offstage, or Lincoln retired from office?
The vogue of the vague, what can it teach an artist?
Beethoven was a Romantic, but too good;
did kings, republics or Napoleon teach him?
He was his own Napoleon. Did even deafness?
Does the painted soldier in the painting bleed?
Is the captive chorus of *Fidelio* bound?
For a good voice hearing is a torture.

79

While Hearing the Archduke Trio

None march in the Archduke's War, or worse lost cause,
without promise of plunder, murder, gallantry.
Marriage is less remunerative than war—
two waspheads lying on one pillowslip,
drowning, one toe just skating the sheet for bedrock.
The bright moonlight mackerels heaven in my garden,
fair flesh of the turtle given shape by shell,
Eve shining like an illuminated rib,
forsaking this garden for another bondage.
I so pray this pretty sky to stay:
my high blood, fireclouds, the first dew,
elms black on the moon, our birdhouse on a pipe. . . .
Was the Archduke, the music-patron, childless? Beethoven
married the single muse, her ear of flint.

Goethe

Goethe thought logical consistency
suited the genius of hypochondriacs,
who take life and art too seriously,
lacking the artist's germ of reckless charm.
"How can I perish, I do not exist. . . .
The more I understand particular things,"
he said, "the more I understand God."
He loathed neurotics for the harm they do,
and fettered *Te deum laudamus* in his meter,
not *pauper amavi*. Take him, he's not copy—
past rationalism and irrationalism,
saved by humor and wearying good health,
hearing his daemon's cold corrosive whisper
chill his continuous ardor for young girls.

Coleridge

Coleridge stands, he flamed for the one friend. . . .
This shower is warm, I almost breathe-in the rain
horseclopping from fire escape to skylight
down to a dungeon courtyard. In April, New York
has a smell and taste of life. For whom . . . what?
A newer younger generation faces
the firing squad, then their blood is wiped from the pavement. . . .
Coleridge's laudanum and brandy,
his alderman's stroll to positive negation—
his passive courage is paralysis,
standing him upright like tenpins for the strike,
only kept standing by a hundred scared habits . . .
a large soft-textured plant with pith within,
power without strength, an involuntary imposter.

Leopardi, The Infinite

That hill pushed off by itself was always dear
to me and the hedges near
it that cut away so much of the final horizon.
When I would sit there lost in deliberation,
I reasoned most on the interminable spaces
beyond all hills,
the silence beyond my possibility.
Here for a little my heart is quiet inside me;
and when the wind lifts roughing through the trees,
I set about comparing my silence to those sounds,
I think about the infinite, the dead seasons,
this one that is present and alive,
the rumors we leave behind us, our small choice . . .
it is sweet to destroy my mind, and drown in this sea.

The Lost Tune

As I grow older, I must admit with terror:
I have been there, the works of the masters lose,
songs with a mind, philosophy that danced.
Their *vivace* clogs, I am too tired, or wise.
I have read in books that even woman dies;
a figure cracks up sooner than a landscape—
your locale was Maine, a black and white engraving,
able to enlarge the formal luxury of
foliage rendered by a microscope,
a thousand blueberry bushes marching up
the flank of a hill; the artist, a lady, shoots
her lover panting like a stag at bay;
not very true, yet art—had Schubert scored it,
and his singer left the greenroom with her voice.

Death and the Maiden

In Romantic painting, the girl is Body,
just as she must embody youth to die;
Death too must take a body to make a scene—
verismo has no tenor for death.
But in music . . . I've been thirty years
hearing the themes of Schubert's *Death and the Maiden*:
Schubert dying is death audible;
which theme is Maiden, which Death—*la femme fatale?*
Death will make melodrama of most of us,
change her chilled, unwilling audience to actors. . . .
These years of my dead friends, still mine—what other possession
allows no aging or devaluation?
Their names have kept their voice—*only in the movies,
the maiden lives . . . in the madness of art.*

Die Forelle

I lean on a bridgerail watching the clear calm,
a homeless sound of joy is in the sky:
a fisherman making falsecasts over a brook,
a two pound browntrout darting with scornful quickness,
drawing straight lines like arrows through the pool.
The man might as well snap his rod on his knee,
each shake of a boot or finger scares the fish;
trout will never hit flies in this brightness.
I go on watching, and the man keeps casting,
he wades, and stamps his feet, and muddies the water;
before I know it, his rod begins to dip.
He wades, he stamps, he shouts to turn the run
of the trout with his wetfly breathed into its belly—
broken whiplash in the gulp of joy.

Heine Dying in Paris 1

Every idle desire has died in my breast;
even hatred of evil things, even care
of my own distress and others.
What lives in me is death.
The curtain falls, the play is done;
my dear German public goes home yawning . . .
these good people—they're no fools—
eat their suppers and drink their glass of wine
quite happily—singing and laughing. . . .
That fellow in Homer's book was right,
he said the meanest little living Philistine
in Stuttgart-am-Neckar is luckier than I,
the golden haired Achilles, the dead lion,
prince of the shadows in the underworld.

My day was luckily happier than my night;
whenever I struck the lyre of inspiration,
my people clapped; my lieder, all joy and fire,
pierced Germany's suffocating summer cloud.
Summer still glows, but my harvest is in the barn,
my sword's scabbarded in my spinal marrow,
and soon I must give up the half-gods
that made my world so agonizingly half-joyful.
My hand clangs to its close on the lyre's dominant;
my insolently raised champagne glass breaks at my lips. . . .
If I can forgive the great Aristophanes
and Author of Being his joke, he can forgive me—
God, how hatefully bitter it is to die,
how snugly one lives in this snug earthly nest!

Old Prints: Decatur, Old Hickory

Those awful figures of Yankee prehistory;
the prints were cheap once, our good faith came easy:
Stephen Decatur, spyglass screwed to raking
the cannonspout-smashed Bay of Tripoli—
because the Mohammedans believed in war.
Our country right or wrong—our commanders had no
commission to send their souls to paradise.
Others were more democratic: primitive, high-toned
President Jackson on his hobby horse,
watermelon-slice hat and ballroom sword;
he might have been the Tsar or Bolivar,
pillar of the right or pillar of the left—
Andrew Jackson, despite appearances,
stands for the gunnery that widened suffrage.

Northwest Savage

"With people like the great silent majority,
how can the great people get elected President?"
St. Paul and Lincoln Nebraska owe their rise
to W. H. Harrison, selfish little busybody
expelling Indians, legalizing slaves,
losing most of his battles with the Savage,
with numbers anything equal. No acid ate more
mechanically on vegetable fibre
than the whites in number. . . . Did the fish leaping
have leisure to see their waters had collapsed,
that even Jefferson's philanthropy
offered a great award for their extinction?
Landthirst, whiskeythirst. We flip extinct matches
at your rhinoceros hide . . . inflammable earth.

Henry and Waldo

Emerson is New England's Montaigne or Goethe,
cold ginger, poison to Don Giovanni—
see him on winter lecture-tours with Thoreau,
red flannels, one bowl of broken ice for shaving;
few lives contained such humdrum renunciations.
Thoreau, like Mallarmé and many others, found life
too brief for perfection, too long for comfort.
His friend would sooner take the arm of an elm,
yet he must have heard the voices on the river,
wood groans, water groans, gliding of bark canoes,
twilight flaking the wild manes of trees.
The color that killed him, us . . . perhaps a mouse,
zinc eating through the moonstalk, or a starling
lighting and pecking, a dash of poisonous metal.

Thoreau 1

God is the figure for environment,
all that I know, all that I fail to know;
who is mightier than the living God?
Other persons only met in books
have swallowed a bad name and made a comeback.
Students return to Othello and Macbeth,
Shakespeare's insomniac self and murderer,
his visionary captain trapped in scandal
by Shiva, the killer and a third of God.
No killer troubled Thoreau on his walk;
he thought never to see the piece of earth
that would bury him. God buried him.
He was forty-five, a good age for the lover;
the maker and destroyer had no quarrel.

Thoreau 2

He thought New England was corrupted by
too much communion with her saints,
our fears consoled and iced, no hope confirmed.
If the high sun wandered and warmed a winter day
and surprised the plodding circuit of our lives,
we winced and called it fickleness and fools-thaw—
"However bad your life, meet it, live it,
it's not as bad as you are." For Thoreau,
life in us was like water in a river:
"It may rise higher this year than all others."
Adrift there, dragging forty feet of line,
he felt a dull, uncertain, blundering purpose
jerking, slow to make up its mind, and knew
the light that blinds our eyes is not the sun.

Margaret Fuller Drowned

You had everything to rattle the men who wrote.
The first American woman? Margaret Fuller . . .
in a white nightgown, your hair fallen long
at the foot of the foremast, you just forty,
your husband Angelo thirty, your Angelino one—
all drowned with brief anguish together. . . . Your fire-call,
your voice, was like thorns crackling under a pot,
you knew the Church burdens and infects as all dead forms,
however gallant and lovely in their life;
progress is not by renunciation.
"Myself," you wrote, "is all I know of heaven.
With my intellect, I always can
and always shall make out, but that's not half—
the life, the life, O my God, will life never be sweet?"

Henry Adams 1850

Adams' connection with Boston was singularly cool;
winter and summer were two hostile lives,
summer was multiplicity, winter was school.
"We went into the pinewoods, netted crabs,
boated the saltmarsh in view of the autumn hills.
Boys are wild animals, I felt nature crudely,
I was a New England boy—summer was drunken,
poled through the saltmarsh at low tide,
the strong reds, greens, purples in children's Bibles—
no light line or color, our light was glare.
Already the Civil War darkened Fanueil Hall.
My refined, disquieting mind, I suppose
it had some function . . . sometimes by mishap
Napoleon's Old Guard were actually used in battle."

Colonel Charles Russell Lowell 1835–64

OCCASIONEM COGNOSCE

Hard to exhume him from our other Union martyrs;
though common now, his long-short, crisping hair,
the wire mustache, and manly, foppish coat—
more and more nearly looking like our sixties student. . . .
Twelve horses killed under him—his nabob cousin
bred and shipped replacements. He had, *gave* . . . everything
at Cedar Creek, his men dismounted, firing
repeating carbines; heading two vicious charges,
a slug collapsing his bad, tubercular lung:
fainting, loss of his voice above a whisper;
his general—any crusader since Moses—shouting:
"I'll sleep in the enemy camp tonight, or hell. . . ."
Charles had himself strapped to the saddle . . . bound to death,
his cavalry that scorned the earth it trod on.

Abraham Lincoln

All day I fence and strike at you in thought,
as if I had the licence of your wife. . . .
Your War was a continuation of politics—
is politics the discontinuation of murder?
You may have loved underdogs and even mankind,
this one thing made you different from your equals . . .
you, our one genius in politics . . . who followed
the bull to the altar . . . death in unity.
J'accuse, j'accuse, j'accuse, j'accuse, j'accuse!
Say it in American. Who shot the deserters?
Winter blows sparks in the face of the new God,
who breathes-in fire and dies with cooling faith,
as the firebrand turns black in the black hand,
and the squealing pig darts sidewise from his foot.

George Eliot

A lady in bonnet, brow clearer than the Virgin,
the profile of a white rhinoceros—
like Emerson, she hated gardens, thinking
a garden is a grave, and drains the inkwell;
she never wished to have a second youth—
as for living, she didn't leave it to her servants,
her union, Victorian England's one true marriage,
one Victorian England pronounced *Mormonage*—
two virgins; they published and were childless. Our writers often
marry writers, are true, bright, clashing, though lacking
this woman's dull gray eyes, vast pendulous nose,
her huge mouth, and jawbone which forbore to finish:
George Eliot with Tolstoy's once inalienable eye,
George Eliot, a Countess Tolstoy . . . without Tolstoy.

Hugo at Théophile Gautier's Grave

I have begun to die by being alone,
I feel the summit's sinister cold breath;
we die. That is the law. None holds it back,
and the great age with all its light departs.
The oaks cut for the pyre of Hercules,
what a harsh roar they make
in the night vaguely breaking into stars—
Death's horses toss their heads, neigh, roll their eyes;
they are joyful because the shining day now dies.
Our age that mastered the high winds and waves
expires. . . . And you, their peer and brother, join
Lamartine, Dumas, Musset. Gautier,
the ancient spring that made us young is dry;
you knew the beautiful, go, find the true.

Baudelaire *1. The Abyss*

Pascal's abyss moved with him as he moved—
all void, alas—activity, desires, words!
above, below me, only space and shoal,
the spaces, the bat-wing of insanity.
I cuddle the insensible blank air,
I envy the void insensibility
and fear to sleep as one fears a great hole.
On my mind the raised hand of the Ultimate
traces his nightmare, truceless, uniform.
I have cultivated this hysteria
with terror and enjoyment till I see
only the infinite at every window,
vague, captivating, dropping who knows where. . . .
Ah never to escape from being and number!

Baudelaire *2. Recollection*

Be calm, my Sorrow, you must move with care.
You asked for evening, it descends, it's here;
Paris is coffined in its atmosphere,
bringing some relief and others care.
Now while the common multitude strips bare,
feels pleasure's cat o'nine tails on its back,
accumulating remorse at the great bazaar—
give me your hand, my Sorrow. Let's stand back,
back from these people. Look, the defunct years, dressed
in period costume crowd the balconies of the sky.
Regret emerges smiling from the river,
the sun, worked overtime, sleeps beneath an arch . . .
and like a long shroud stretched from east to west—
listen, my Dearest, hear the sweet night march!

Rimbaud 1. Bohemia

I walked on the great roads, my two fists lost
in my coat's slashed pockets; my overcoat too
was the ghost of a coat. Under the sky—
I was your student, Muses. What an affair
we had together! My only trousers were a big hole.
Tom Thumb, the stargazer. I brightened my steps with rhymes.
My inn was at the Sign of the Great Bear;
the stars sang like silver in my hands.
I listened to them and squatted on my heels,
September twilights and September twilights,
rhyming into the monster-crowded dark,
the rain splashing on my face like cheap wine.
I plucked the elastics on my clobbered boots
like lyrestrings, one foot squeezed tight against my heart.

Rimbaud 2. A Knowing Girl

In the cigar-brown dining room perfumed
with a smell of fruitbowls and shellac,
I was wolfing my plate of God knows what
Belgian dish. I sprawled in a huge chair,
I listened to the clock tock while I ate.
Then the kitchen door opened with a bang,
the housemaid came in . . . who knows why . . . her blouse
half-open and her hair wickedly set. She passed
her little finger trembling across her cheek,
pink and white peach bloom, and made a grimace
with her childish mouth, and coming near me
tidied my plates to make me free . . .
then—just like that, to get a kiss of course—
whispered, "Feel this, my cheek has caught a cold."

Rimbaud 3. Sleeper in the Valley

The river sings and cuts a hole in the meadow,
madly hooking white tatters on the rushes.
Light escalades the strong hills. The small
valley bubbles with sunbeams like a beerglass.
The young conscript bareheaded and open-mouthed,
his neck cooling in blue watercress;
he's sleeping. The grass soothes his heaviness,
the sunlight is raining in his green bed,
baking away the aches of his body. He smiles,
as a sick child might smile himself asleep.
O Nature, rock him warmly, he is cold.
The fields no longer make his hot eyes weep.
He sleeps in the sun, a hand on his breast lies open,
at peace. He has two red holes in his left side.

Rimbaud 4. The Evil

All day the red spit of the grapeshot smears
whistling across the infinite blue sky;
before the Emperor, in blue and scarlet,
the massed battalions flounder into fire.
The criminal folly that conspires and rules us
lays a hundred thousand corpses end on end—
O Nature, in your summer, your grass, your joy—
you made them, these poor dead men, in holiness! . . .
There's a God who laughs at damask altarcloths,
the great gold chalice, the fuming frankincense.
He dozes exhausted through our grand hosannah,
and wakes when mothers, brought together in pain,
and weeping underneath their old black hat,
give him the big penny they tied in their handkerchief.

Rimbaud 5. Napoleon after Sedan

(Rimbaud, the servant of the France he saved,
feared the predestined flow of his aesthetic
energies was to use the wrong direction;
he was looking for writing he needn't hate—)
Napoleon is waxy, and walks the barrack's unflowering
garden, a black cigar between his teeth . . .
a hand once able to stub out liberty.
His twenty years orgy has made him drunk.
Liberty jogs on, the great man stands,
he's captured. O what name is quaking on
his lip? What plebiscites? What Robespierre?
His shark's eye on the horses, the Grand Prix,
soirées at Saint Cloud, their manly vapor . . .
watching his cigar blue out in smoke.

La Lumière

In the blur of my glasses, you cannot fade—
your ruffle, electricity and your sure tongue . . .
richer now and much more radical.
The sun lights your windows it will never crash,
this blind snow, this blind light everywhere,
the sad, metallic sunlight of New York
throwing light on something about to die.
This light was familiar in the older cities;
it goes, disclosing less than leaves of artichokes—
a light that blinded kings who fled to London,
where Dickens might have played Napoleon's Nephew
cloaked in cigar smoke and the moans of girls,
a smell of chestnuts like a humidor . . .
watching exile chew his face from the mirror.

Mallarmé 1. Swan

Does the virgin, the alive, the beautiful day
dare tear for us with a mad stroke of its wing
the hard, neglectful lake hoarding under ice
a great glacier of flights that never fly?
The swan ruffles, remembers it is he,
fortitude that finds no raison d'être,
magnificence that gives itself no hope,
for never singing the country where one lives—
the great boredom blazing on sterile winter.
His whole neck shakes in his white agony
inflicted by the space the swan denies,
the horror of the ice that ties his wings,
the brilliance that led him to this grand asylum,
governed by staccato cries of grandeur.

Mallarmé 2. Gift of a Poem

I bring the child of an Idumean night,
a black thing bleeding, stumbling—its wings are plucked.
Through the window's gold and aromatic fire,
panes frosted by night, alas, and wearisome,
the dawn throws itself upon my sacred lamp—
palms! It reveals this relic to its father;
I try to cheer it with a hostile smile
that chills our blue and sterile solitude.
Nurse, Mother, with our child's innocence
and your cold feet, welcome this monster birth—
your voice is like viol and harpsichord.
Will your wilting fingers press a breast
flowing with solid whiteness, bringing woman
to lips the virgin azure has made hungry?

94

Main Street

They were talking much as usual only
laughing, talking rather too much and louder;
they had hoisted poplar trees to the people,
and the head of state with the head of a pig.
There was a lot of unclaimed space around.
The teenage police shook with chills-and-fever;
behind them, veterans of Sedan and Metz
fixed starry bayonets. It didn't look like a killing.
Like a dark worm, the eight-foot barricade;
a small mongrel with pipecleaner legs trots the top.
Joy! Indescribable apprehension. House-arrest
for women, children, foreigners and dogs.
Red-trousered, unpressed fatigues, the Communards
stand like empty wine-bottles on the table.

Lady Cynthia Asquith, 1916

(WRITTEN IN ISRAEL 1969)

"I am beginning to rub my eyes at the prospect of peace,
when we will have to know the dead are not
dead only for the duration of the war;
I am in glowing looks, I've never seen
myself in such keen color, even by daylight.
Strange to know suddenly in this slowly farewell war
that I know many more dead than I know living. . . ."
Turning the page in *Time* to see her picture,
I expect some London Judith: *no trespass.*
I touch your shutter-green sweater and breathing breasts:
Lady Cynthia Asquith, undying bulwark of British girl. . . .
Miracles were more common once than now,
but sleeping with this one can not be maneuvered—
each stone a wall, an unexploded minefield.

Verdun

I bow down to the great goiter of Verdun,
I know what's buried there, ivory telephone,
ribs, hips bleached to parchment, a pale machinegun—
they lie fatigued from too much punishment,
cling by a string to friends they knew first-hand,
to the God of our fathers still twenty like themselves.
Their medals and rosettes have kept in bloom,
they stay young, only living makes us age.
I know the sort of town they came from, straight brownstone,
each house cooled by a rectilinear private garden,
a formal greeting and a slice of life.
The city says, "I am the finest city"—
landmass held by half a million bodies
for Berlin and Paris, twin cities saved at Verdun.

Hospital

We're lost if gossip is taken for gospel truth,
worse lost if we have found no truth in gossip—
we must take courses in what's alive and what isn't,
trips to the hospital. . . . I have seen stiffs
no one can distinguish from the living,
twitched by green fingers till they turn to flowers;
they are and are not—like the unknown soldier,
his archaic statue no barrage will wake. . . .
Others are strapped to cots, thrust out in hallways,
they are browner and flatter than we are,
they are whatever crinkles, plugged to tubes
plugged in jugs of dim blue doctored water,
a yard above them to lift their eyes to heaven—
they look dead, unlike the hero, and are alive.

96

Revenants

They come back sometimes, I know they do,
freed like felons on the first of May,
if there's a healthy bite in the south wind,
Spring the echo of God's single day.
They sun like earthworms on the puddly mall,
they are better equipped for everything than people,
except perhaps for living. When I meet them
covertly, I think I know their names:
Cousin So, Ancestral Mother-in-Law So . . .
I cannot laugh them into laughing back.
"Dead we have finally come to realize
what others must have known from infancy—
God is not about. We are less scared—
with misty bounds we scale the starry sheer."

Cadet-Picture of Rilke's Father

There's absence in the eyes. The brow's in touch
with something far, and his enormous mouth,
tempted, serious, is a boy's unsmiling . . .
modest, counting on future promotion, stiff
in his slender aristocratic uniform—
both hands bulge on the basket-hilt of his saber.
They are quiet and reach out to nothing.
I can hardly see them now, as if
they were the first to grasp distance and disappear.
All the rest is curtained in itself,
and so faded I cannot understand
my father as he bleaches on this page—
You quickly disappearing daguerreotype
in my more slowly disappearing hand.

97

Annensky: White Winter, Black Spring

Half-holiday for the burial. Of course we punished
our provincial copper bells for hours.
Terribly the nose tilted up like a tallow candle
from the coffin. Does he want
to draw breath from his torso in its morning suit?
We did not blow the candles until morning.
The snow fell somberly—now the roads are breadcrumbs.
Goodbye, poor winter honeycombed with debts—
now numb black spring looks at the chilly eye.
From under the mould on the roof shingles,
the liquid oatmeal of the roads,
the green stubble on our faces—life . . . in splinter elms
shrill the annual fledgelings with spikey necks.
They say to man his road is mud, or nothing.

Under the Tsar

No beer or washrag, half the lightbulbs bust,
still the baths are free, a treat for kings,
rows of tubs like churchpews infinite,
on each a reading-board, a pair of glasses,
a cake of scouring soap, and Marx in French.
When we have read our bible, we are washed—
the dirt of a lifetime cleaned from our fingernails;
our breasts, as the sons of Belial dreamed, are chests,
we are like our backs. We, who were wet and cold,
soak . . . dry for the first time in our lives.
But our hurt gums still leave a smear of blood on the apple;
we can't do all things, drink the spit of the snake
and meet the naked candor of the Tsar,
his slightly bald Medusa's pewter eye.

Romanoffs

Let's face it, English is a racist last ditch.
We plead guilty, the laws of history tell us
irrelevant things that happen never happened.
The Blacks and Reds survive, but who is White?
The word has fallen from the English tongue,
a class wiped out, their legacy, non-existence.
The new blade is too sharp, the old poisons.
Does arrogance give the ruler solitude
to study the desolation of his thought—
the starred cellar, where they shot and then dismembered
Tsar, Tsarina, the costly hemophilic children—
"Those *statesmen*," said Lenin, "sent 16 million to death."
Such fairy stories beguiled our brainwashed youth—
we, the Romanoffs with much to lose.

Dispossession

The paint is always peeling from the palace—
a man of eighty with the leg of iron,
striding fields shaved smooth as a putting green.
I see these far fields as easily as the present. . . .
How many of the enthusiasts are gone;
their strapped legs march, their impudent white standards
droop in the dust of the field, the gas of battle . . .
and the heart's moisture goes up like summer drought.
No passkey jingles on the sky's blue smoke-ring. . . .
The firemen smash holes in their own house;
yet dispossession isn't entirely our answer,
we yearn to swoop with the swallow's brute joy,
indestructible as mercy—round green weed
slipping free from the disappointment of the flower.

Rilke Self-Portrait

An old, long-noble people's unregressing
knack of holding is in the build of the eyebrow;
a scared blue child is peering through the eyes,
that now and then are humble like a woman's,
not servile . . . on occasion glad to serve.
A mouth made like a mouth, largish, in place,
less good at persuasion than for saying things.
Nothing wrong with the brow; it seldom frowns,
at home with quiet shadows, or looking down. . . .
As a thing that hangs together, the picture fails;
nothing is worked through yet or alive,
carried to enduring culmination—
as if hidden in accidents and stray things,
something unassailable were planned.

Muses of George Grosz

Berlin in the twenties left the world behind,
the iron glove of Prussia was unclenched,
elsewhere the music crept, and painting stank—
now our artists hurry to break windows,
as if we had beaten Germany at last.
Grosz' men are one man, old Marshal Hindenberg,
a close-cropped Midas feeling girls to gold.
His men never strip, his women always;
girls one meets at a Modern Language Annual,
pushing retirement, and outweighing men;
once the least of them were good for the game all night.
Grosz could swing the old sow by her tits:
the receding hairline of her nettled cunt
caught like a scalplock by a stroke of the brush.

The Poet

His teeth splayed in a way he'd notice and pity
in his closest enemies or friends.
Youth held his eye; he blinked at passing beauties,
birds of passage that could not close the gap.
His wife was high-blooded, he counted on her living—
she lived, past sixty, then lived on in him,
and often when he plotted lines, she breathed
her acrid sweetness past his imaginings.
She was still a magnificent handle of a woman—
did she have her lover as a novelist wished her?
No—hating someone nearer, she found her voice—
no wife so loved; though Hardy, home from cycling,
was glad to climb unnoticed to his study
by a circling outside staircase, his own design.

Scar-Face

By Lake Erie, Al Capone could set
his price on the moonshine that enflamed Chicago—
"Funny thing, in this our thing, a man
in this line of business has too much company."
He watched black and white men walk the tightrope,
and felt a high contempt for them all—poor fish,
sweating themselves to death for a starvation wage.
Little Caesar, like Julius Caesar, a rich man
knifed by richer. A true king serves the realm,
when he's equal to the man who serves his meal;
a gentleman is an aristocrat on bail. . . .
Splendor spread like gold leaf in your hand, Al,
made in the morning and by midday hard,
pushed by your fellow convicts to the wall.

Little Millionaire's Pad, Chicago

The little millionaire's is a sheen of copies;
at first glance most everything is French;
a sonata scored *sans rigueur*
is on a muddy-white baby grand piano,
the little plaster bust on it, small as a medallion,
is Franz Schubert below the colored blow-up
of the master's wife, executive-Bronzino—
his frantic touch to antique her! Out the window,
two cunning cylinder apartment towers—
below the apartments, six spirals of car garage,
below the cars, yachts at moorings—more Louis Quinze
and right than anything of the millionaire's,
except the small daughter's bedroom, perfect with posters:
"Do not enter. Sock it to me, Baby."

Wolverine, *1927*

What did I know about the wolverine,
the Canada of Ernest Seton Thompson,
first great snow in the schoolbook, a Cartesian blank?
At the edge of the rumpled sky, a too-red glow,
a vertical iron rail, derrick or steeple,
trappers freighting on snowshoes through the snow,
track of the wolfpack wheelsaw to the church—
no need for preachers to tell me wolves eat meat,
improve the terror of the first trapped wolf. . . .
The wolverine, no critic of frontier justice,
learning the jaws meant him, was greatly tested,
hestitating to chew off his foot,
tasting the leisure of his double-choice . . .
our first undated leap in evolution.

Two Farmers

A nose flat-bent, no brave, cheeks razored wood—
Velasquez' self-portrait is James MacDonald,
Jim to grandfather, MacDonald to the children,
though always *Mr.* in our vocative.
Having a farmer then was like owning a car . . .
he sits on his lawn waiting a lift to the Old Men's Home—
saying? Here even the painter's speaking likeness fails;
nor could he paint my grandfather. I've overtaken
most of the elders of my youth, not this one,
yet I begin to feel why Grandpa knelt in the snow
so many weekends with his small grandson
sawing his cordwood for a penny a log—
Old Cato, ten years to live, preferring this squander
to his halcyon Roman credits from the Boom.

The Well

The stones of the well were sullenly unhewn,
none could deny their leechlike will to stay—
no dwelling near and four square miles of waste,
pale grass diversified by wounds of sand,
weeds as hard as rock and squeezed by winter,
each well-stone an illrounded ostrich egg,
amateurish for nature's artless hand . . .
a kind of dead chimney. Any furtive boy
was free to pitch the bucket, drinking glass
and funnel down the well . . . thin black hoops
of standing water. That well is bottomless;
plenty of elbowroom for the scuttled gear,
room at bottom for us to lie, undented. . . .
It's not the crowds, but crowding kills the soul.

First Things

Nothing worse could happen, life's insecure,
child's fears mostly a fallacious dream;
days one like the other let you live:
up at seven-five, to bed at nine,
the absolving repetitions, the three meals,
the nutritive, unimaginative dayschool meal,
laughing like breathing, one night's sleep a day—
solitude is the reward for sickness:
leafless, dusty February trees,
the field fretted in your window, all one cloth—
your mother harrowed by child gaiety. . . .
I remember that first calendar with fear;
something made so much of me lose ground,
the irregular and certain flight to art.

First Love

Two grades above me, though two inches shorter,
Leon Straus, sixthgrade fullback, his reindeer shirt—
passion put a motor in my heart.
I pretended he lived in the house across the street.
In first love a choice is seldom and blinding:
acres of whitecaps strew that muddy swell,
old crap and white plastic jugs lodge on shore.
Later, we learn better places to cast
our saffron sperm, and grasp what wisdom fears,
breasts stacked like hawknests in her boyfriend's shirt,
thing a deft hand tips on its back with a stick. . . .
Is it refusal of error breaks our life—
the supreme artist, Flaubert, was a boy before
the mania for phrases enlarged his heart.

1930's I

The vaporish closeness of this two-month fog;
forty summers back, my brightest summer:
the rounds of Dealer's Choice, the housebound girls,
fog, the nightlife. Then, as now, the late curfew
boom of an unknown nightbird, local hemlock
gone black as Roman cypress, the barn-garage
below the tilted Dipper lighthouse-white,
a single misanthropic frog complaining
from the water hazard on the shortest hole;
till morning! Long dreams, short nights; their faces flash
like burning shavings, scattered bait and ptomaine
caught by the gulls with groans like straining rope;
windjammer pilgrims cowled in yellow hoods,
gone like the summer in their yellow bus.

Searching

I look back to you, and cherish what I wanted:
your flashing superiority to failure,
hair of yellow oak leaves, the arrogant
tanned brunt in the snow-starch of a loosened shirt—
your bullying half erotic rollicking. . . .
The white bluffs rise above the old rock piers,
wrecked past insuring by two hurricanes.
As a boy I climbed those scattered blocks and left
the sultry Sunday seaside crowd behind,
seeking landsend, with my bending fishing rod
a small thread slighter than the dark arc of your eyebrow. . . .
Back at school, alone and wanting you,
I scratched my four initials, R.T.S.L.
like a dirty word across my bare, blond desk.

Shake of the electric fan above our village;
oil truck, refrigerator, or just men,
nightly reloading of the village flesh—
plotting worse things than marriage. They found dates
wherever summer is, the nights of the swallow
clashing in heat, storm-signal to stay home.
At night the lit blacktop fussing like a bosom;
Court Street, Dyer Lane, School, Green, Main Street
dropping through shade-trees to the shadeless haven—
young girls are white as ever. I only know
their mothers, sweatshirts gorged with tennis balls,
still air expiring from the tilting bubble—
I too wore armor, strode riveted in cloth,
stiff, a broken clamshell labeled man.

Joe Wardwell: Mink

In the unspoiled age, when they caught a cow-mink,
they made her urinate around the traps,
and every bull-mink hunting along the stream
went for the trap, and soon the mink were done—
the last we knew was in the freeze of '17,
a last bull making tracks in the snow for a last cow.
My friend, once professional, no longer traps:
"There're too many other ways to make a living"—
his, his army pension, and two working sons.
He builds houses for bluebirds, martins, swallows.
When a pair mates in one, it's like a match,
a catch, a return to his lost craft of trapping,
old China's hope to excel without progress. . . .
His money went to *Wildlife*; he killed too much.

1930's 3

The boys come, each year more gallant, playing chicken,
then braking to a standstill for a girl—
like bullets hitting bottles, spars and gulls,
echoing and ricochetting across the bay . . .
hardy perennials! Kneedeep in the cowpond,
far from this cockfight, cattle stop to watch us,
and having had their fill, go back to lapping
soiled water indistinguishable from heaven.
Cattle get onto living, but to *live*:
Kokoschka at eighty, saying, "If you last,
you'll see your reputation die three times,
or even three cultures; young girls are always here."
They *were* there . . . two fray-winged dragonflies,
clinging to a thistle, too clean to mate.

1930's 4

My legs hinge on my foreshortened bathtub
small enough for Napoleon's marching tub. . . .
The sun sallows a tired swath of balsam needles,
the color soothes, and yet the scene confines;
sun falls on so many, many other things:
Custer, leaping with his wind-gold scalplock,
half a furlong or less from the Sioux front line,
and Sitting Bull, who sent our rough riders under—
both now dead drops in the decamping mass. . . .
This wizened balsam, the sea-haze of blue gauze,
the distance plighting a tree-lip of land to the islands—
who can cash a check on solitude,
or is more loved for being distant . . . love-longing
mists my windshield, soothes the eye with milk.

Bobby Delano

The labor to breathe that younger, rawer air:
St. Mark's last football game with Groton lost on the ice-crust,
the sunlight gilding the golden polo coats
of boys with country seats on the Upper Hudson.
Why does that stale light stay? First Form hazing,
first day being sent on errands by an oldboy,
Bobby Delano, cousin of Franklin Delano Roosevelt—
deported soused off the Presidential yacht
baritoning *You're the cream in my coffee* . . .
his football, hockey, baseball letter at 15;
at 15, expelled. He dug my ass with a compass,
forced me to say "My mother is a whore."
My freshman year, he shot himself in Rio,
odious, unknowable, inspired as Ajax.

1930's 5

Timid in victory, chivalrous in defeat,
almost, almost. . . . I bow and watch the ashes
reflect the heraldry of an age less humbled,
though hardened with its nobles, serfs and faith—
(my once faith?) The fires men build live after them,
this night, this night, I elfking, I stonehands sit
feeding the wildfire wildrose of the fire
clouding the cottage window with my lust's
alluring emptiness. I hear the moon
simmer the mildew on a pile of shells,
the fruits of my banquet . . . a boiled lobster,
red shell and hollow foreclaw, cracked, sucked dry,
flung on the ash-heap of a soggy carton—
it eyes me, two pinhead, burnt-out popping eyes.

1930's 6

Months of it, and the inarticulate mist so thick
we turned invisible to one another
across our silence . . . rivals unreconciled,
each unbandaging a tender bloodsoaked foot
in the salmon-glow of the early lighted moon,
snuffed by the malodorous and frosty murk. . . .
Then the iron bellbuoy is rocking like a baby,
the high tide turning on its back exhausted—
colored, dreaming, silken spinnakers
flash in patches through the island pine,
like vegetating millennia of lizards
fed on fern or cropping at the treetops,
straw-chewers in the African siesta.
I never thought scorn of things; struck fear in no man.

1930's 7

The shore was pebbled with eroding brick,
seaweed in grizzling furrows—a surf-cast away,
a converted brickyard dormitory; higher,
the blacktop; higher yet, *The Osprey Nest*,
a bungalow, view-hung and staring, with washing
and picture-window. Whatever we cast out
takes root—weeds shoot up to litter overnight,
sticks of dead rotten wood in drifts, the fish
with a missing eye, or heel-print on the belly,
or a gash in the back from a stray hook—
roads, lawns and harbor stitched with motors,
yawl-engine, outboard, power mower, plowing
the mangle and mash of the monotonous frontier—
when the mower stopped clanking, sunset calmed the ocean.

For Archie Smith 1917–35

(KILLED IN A CAR WRECK)

Our sick elms rise to breathe the peace of heaven,
at six the blighting leaves are green as mint,
the tree shadows blacker than trunk or branch—
Main Street's shingled mansards and square white frames
date from Warren G. Harding back to Adams—
old life! America's ghostly innocence.
I pipe-dream of a summer without a Sunday,
its steerage drive with children and Cousin Belle. . . .
I have driven when I ought not to have driven.
When cars were horse and buggy and roads dirt,
Smith made Sarasota from Princeton in three days.
A good fast driver is like the Lord unsleeping,
he never kills and he is never killed;
when he dies, a friend is always driving.

For Frank Parker 1. 1935

She never married, because she liked to talk,
"You watch the waves *woll* and *woll* and *woll* and *woll*,"
Miss Parker lisped. That's how we found Nantucket.
Wave-watching bored us, though we tried the surf,
hung dead on its moment of infinity,
corked between water, gravel and the gulls, smothered,
smitten from volition. When I breathe now,
I sometimes hear a far pant of gulls in my chest,
but death that summer was our classmate killed
in a wreck at Oak Bluffs near us . . . the first in our form. . . .
In your seascape Moses broke the Ten Commandments
on a shore of saltgrass, dune and surf,
repainted and repainted, till the colors aged,
a whirl of mud in the hand of Michelangelo.

110

For Frank Parker 2

The *Pisspot*, our sailing dory, could be moved
by sail and oar in tune . . . immovable
by either singly. The ocean died. We rocked
debating who was skipper, then shipped oars;
as we drifted I tried to put our rapture in verse:
When sunset rouged the sun-embittered surf.
This was the nearest we got to Melville's Nantucket,
though we'd been artist cottagers a month. . . .
The channel gripped our hull, we could not veer,
the boat swam shoreward flying our wet shirts,
like a birchlog shaking off loose bark and shooting:
And the surf thundered fireworks on the dunes.
This was the moment to choose, as school warned us,
whether to wreck or ride in tow to port.

1930's 8

"Nature never will betray us," the poet swore,
choosing peeled staff, senility and psalter
to scrounge Northumberland for the infinite. . . .
We burned the sun of the universal bottle,
and summered on a shorefront—the dusk seal
nightly dog-paddling on the hawk for fish,
whiskering the giddy harbor, a black blanket
splotched with spangles of the sky, the sky—
and somewhere the Brook Trout dolphin by the housepiles,
grow common by mid-vacation as hamburger,
fish-translucence cooked to white of an egg. . . .
Summer vacations surround the college winter,
the reach of nature is longer than a car—
I am no bigger than the shoe I fit.

The circular moon saw-wheels through the oak-grove;
below it, clouds . . . permanence of the clouds,
many as have drowned in the Atlantic.
It makes one larger to sleep with the sublime;
the Great Mother shivers under the dead oak—
such cures the bygone Reichian prophets swore to,
such did as gospel for their virgin time—
two elements were truants: man and nature.
By sunrise, the sky is nearer. Strings of fog,
such as we haven't seen in fifteen months,
catch shyly over stopping lobster boats—
smoke-dust the Chinese draftsman made eternal.
His brushwork wears; the hand decayed. A hand does—
we can have faith, at least, the hand decayed.

Anne Dick 1. 1936

Father's letter to your father said
stiffly and much too tersely he'd been told
you visited my college rooms alone—
I can still crackle that slight note in my hand.
I see your pink father—you, the outraged daughter.
That morning nursing my dark, quiet fire
on the empty steps of the Harvard Fieldhouse in
vacation . . . saying the start of *Lycidas* to myself
fevering my mind and cooling my hot nerves—
we were nomad quicksilver and drove to Boston;
I knocked my father down. He sat on the carpet—
my mother calling from the top of the carpeted stairs,
their glass door locking behind me, no cover; you
idling in the station wagon, no retreat.

Anne Dick 2. 1936

Longer ago than I had lived till then . . .
before the *Anschluss*, the ten or twenty million
war-dead . . . but who knows now off-hand how many?
I wanted to marry you, we gazed through your narrow
bay window at the hideous concrete dome
of M.I.T., its last blanched, hectic glow
sunsetted on the bay of the Esplanade:
like the classical seaport done by Claude,
an artist more out of fashion now than Nero,
his heaven-vaulting aqueducts, swords forged from plowshares,
the fresh green knife of his unloved mother's death. . . .
The blood of our spirit dries in veins of brickdust—
Christ lost, our only king without a sword,
turning the word *forgiveness* to a sword.

Father

There was rebellion, Father, and the door was slammed.
Front doors were safe with glass then . . . you fell backward
on your heirloom-clock, the phases of the moon,
the highboy quaking to its toes. My Father . . .
I haven't lost heart to say *I knocked you down.* . . .
I have breathed the seclusion of the life-tight den,
card laid on card until the pack is used,
old Helios turning the houseplants to blondes,
moondust blowing in the prowling eye—
a parental sentence on each step misplaced. . . .
You were further from Death than I am now—
that Student ageless in her green cloud of hash,
her bed a mattress half a foot off floor . . .
as far from us as her young breasts will stretch.

Mother and Father 1

Though the clock half-stopped in 1936
for them, then forever in 50 and 54,
they still are . . . until death stops me too,
and the blood of our spirit is out of mind.
They say, "I had my life when I was young."
They must have . . . dying young in middleage;
often the old grow still more beautiful,
watering out the hours, biting back their tears,
as the white moon streams in on them unshaded;
old women also, those tanning roses, their ebb
past psychiatrist or the Gardener. . . .
I hit my father. My apology
scratched the surface of his invisible
coronary . . . never to be effaced.

Mother and Father 2

This glorious oversleeping half through Sunday,
the sickroom's crimeless mortuary calm,
reprieved from leafing through the Sunday papers,
my need as a reader to think celebrities
are made for suffering, and suffer well. . . .
I remember flunking all courses but Roman history—
a kind of color-blindness made the world gray,
though a third of the globe was painted red for Britain. . . .
I think of all the ill I do and will;
love hits like the *infantile* of pre-Salk days.
I always went too far—few children can love,
or even bear their bearers, the never forgotten
my father, *my* mother . . . these names, this function, given
by them once, given existence now by me.

Returning

If, Mother and Daddy, you were to visit us
still seeing you as beings, you'd not be welcome,
as you sat here groping the scars of the house,
spangling reminiscence with reproach,
cutting us to shades you used to skim from Freud—
that first draft lost and never to be rewritten.
No one like one's mother and father ever lived;
when I see my children, I see them only
as children, only-children like myself.
Mother and Father, I try to receive you
as if you were I, as if I were you,
trying to laugh at my old nerveracking jokes . . .
a young, unlettered couple who want to leave—
childhood, closer to me than what I love.

Mother, 1972

More than once taking both roads one night
to shake the inescapable hold of New York—
now more than before fearing everything I do
is only (only) a mix of mother and father,
no matter how unlike they were, they are—
it's not what you were or thought, but you . . .
the choked oblique joke, the weighty luxurious stretch.
Mother, we are our true selves in the bath—
a cold splash each morning, the long hot evening loll.
O dying of your cerebral hemorrhage,
lost at Rapallo, dabbing your brow a week,
bruised from stumbling to your unceasing baths,
as if you hoped to drown your killer wound—
to keep me safe a generation after your death.

Father in a Dream

We were at the faculty dining table,
Freudianizing gossip . . . not of our world;
you wore your Sunday white ducks and blue coat
seeming more in character than life.
At our end of the table, I spattered gossip,
shook salt on my wine-spill; soon we were alone,
suddenly I was talking to you alone.
Your hair, grown heavier, was peacocked out in bangs;
"I do it," you said, "to be myself . . . or younger.
I'll have to make a penny for our classes:
calc and Kipling, and catching small-mouth bass."
Age had joined us at last in the same study.
"I have never loved you so much in all my life."
You answered, "Doesn't love begin at the beginning?"

To Daddy

I think, though I didn't believe it, you were my airhole,
and resigned perhaps from the Navy to be an airhole—
that Mother not warn me to put my socks on before my shoes.

Joan Dick at Eighty

"I opened, I shed bright musk . . . for eighty years?
I've lost the charms of a girl to charm the dragon,
the old flame-thrower dancing rounds to scatter fire. . . .
In my sleep last night, I was on a burning barge,
the angry water was calling me below;
it was jumping or dying at my post.
I had clasped you in my hands, I woke so—
who is washed white in the deep blue sea?
I have spent too much life travelling
from sister to sister each time they felt *down*;
they could never do with God, or without Him—
O His ears that hear not, His mouth that says not . . .
life never comes to us with both hands full;
the tree God touches hears the other trees."

Will Not Come Back

(VOLVERAN)

Dark swallows will doubtless come back killing
the injudicious nightflies with a clack of the beak;
but these that stopped full flight to see your beauty
and my good fortune . . . as if they knew our names—
they'll not come back. The thick lemony honeysuckle,
climbing from the earthroot to your window,
will open more beautiful blossoms to the evening;
but these . . . like dewdrops, trembling, shining, falling,
the tears of day—they'll not come back. . . .
Some other love will sound his fireword for you
and wake your heart, perhaps, from its cool sleep;
but silent, absorbed, and on his knees,
as men adore God at the altar, as I love you—
don't blind yourself, you'll not be loved like that.

Second Shelley

The ceiling is twenty feet above our heads;
oak mantel, panels, oak linoleum tiles;
the book-ladders, brass rods on rollers, touch heaven—
in middle age, necessity costs more. . . .
Who can deduct these years? Become a student,
breathing rebellion, the caw and hair of Shelley,
his hectic hopes, his tremulous success—
dying, he left the wind behind him.
Here, the light of anarchy would harden in his eyes;
soon he starves his genius for denial,
thinks a clink in the heating, the chirp of birds,
and turns with the tread of an ox to serve the rich,
trusting his genius and a hand from his father
will lift his feet from the mud of the republic.

Ford Madox Ford

Taking Ford's dictation on Samuel Butler
in longhand: "A novelist has one novel, his own."
He swallowed his words, I garbled each seventh word—
"You have no ear," he said, "for civilized prose,
Shakespeare's best writing: *No king, be his cause never so spotless,
will try it out with all unspotted soldiers*."
I brought him my loaded and overloaded lines.
He said: "You live a butterfly's existence,
flitting, flying, botching inspiration.
Conrad spent a day finding the *mot juste*; then killed it."
Ford doubted I could live and be an artist.
"Most of them are born to fill the graveyards."
Ford wrote my father, "If he fails as a writer, at least
he'll be head of Harvard or your English Ambassador."

118

Ford Madox Ford and Others

Ford could pick up talent from the flyspeck,
and had Goethe's gift for picking a bright girl;
most old masters only know themselves:
"The sun rises," they say, "and the sun sets;
what matters is our writing and reviews."
A joyful weariness cushions the worn-out chair,
one flight of stairs, one view of the one tree,
a heater more attentive than a dog—
praise, the last drink for the road, last welcome friend,
when we have buried all our enemies,
and lonely must descend to loneliness,
pronounce through our false teeth, affirm, eyes closed,
the sky above, the moral law within,
answering requests and plotting endless walks.

For Peter Taylor 1

On the great day, when the eyelid of life lifts—
why try to hide it? When we were at Kenyon,
Ezra Pound wrote me, "Amy Lowell
is no skeleton in anybody's closet."
Red leaves embered in the blue cool of fall,
the days we hoped to meet the Ohio girl,
beery, corny, the seductive verb,
mouth like a twat, vagina like a jaw,
small-mouth bass taking three hooks at a strike. . . .
We lost our fiancés on our first drive East—
stood-up by our girls in a wrong restaurant,
spare change ringing like sleighbells in our pockets—
fulfilling the prophecy of my first prize,
my nature cup for catching moths and snakes.

For Peter Taylor 2

Your doleful Kenyon snapshot—ham-squatting in bed,
jaw a bent lantern, your eyes too glossy;
chest syrups, wicked greens of diesel oil;
you the same green, except you are transparent.
At fifty, I can almost touch and smell
the pyjamas we were too sluttish to change,
and wore as winter underwear in our trousers,
thinking cleanliness was ungodliness.
You might have been sitting for your embalmer,
sitting upright, a First Dynasty mummy. . . .
You survive life's obliquities of health, though Adams
knew the Southerner, even as an animal, will lose.
Love teases. We're one still, shakier, wilder—
stuck in one room again, we want to fight.

To Allen Tate 1. 1937

My longest drive, two hundred miles, it seemed:
Nashville to Clarksville to the Cumberland,
March 1937, in *my* month Pisces,
Europe's last fling of impotence and anger—
above your fire the blood-crossed flag of the States,
a print of Stonewall Jackson, your shotgun half-cocked . . .
to shatter into the false windmills of the age.
The cornwhisky was whiter than the purest water;
you told dirty, stately setpieces in Cumberland patois;
you said your tenant with ten children had more art
than Merrill Moore. "Do they expect me to leave the South
to meet frivolous people like Tugwell and Mrs. Roosevelt?"
Ford, playing Russian Banker in the half-light, nagging,
"Don't show your cards, my dear Tate . . . it isn't done."

To Allen Tate 2. 1960's

On your enormous brow, a snowman's knob,
a ripped red tissuepaper child's birthday hat;
you squint, make out my daughter, then six or seven:
"*You* are a Southern *belle*; do you know why
you are a *Southern* belle?" (Stare, stupor, thumb in her mouth)
"Because your *mother* is a Southern belle."
Your eye wanders. "I love you now, but I'll love you
more probably when you are older." Harriet mutters,
"If you are still alive." We reach Gettysburg;
both too much the soldier from the Sourmash:
"I don't know whether to call you my son or my brother."
Ashtrays and icecubes deploy as Pickett's columns:
his flashing forest of slanting steel. You point:
"There, if Longstreet had *moved*, we would have *broke* you."

To Allen Tate 3. Michael Tate August 1967–July 1968

Each night, a star, gold-on-black, a muskellunge,
dies in the highest sphere that never dies. . . .
Things no longer usable for our faith
go on routinely possible in nature;
the worst is the child's death. Even his small gravestone.
the very, very old one, one century gone, two,
his *one-year* common as grass in auld lang syne
is beyond our scale of faith . . . and Michael Tate
gagging on your plastic telephone,
while the new sitter drew water for your bath,
unable to hear you gasp—they think: if there'd been
a week or two's illness, we might have been prepared.
Your twin crawls for you, ten-month twin . . . no longer
young enough to understand what happened.

121

To *Allen Tate* *4.* *A Letter from Allen Tate*

This winter to watch the child of your old age;
and write, "He is my captor. As a young man,
I was too alert to let myself enjoy
Nancy's infancy as I do the little boy's."
Ah that was the mosses ago in your life, mine;
no New York flights this season. "As you must guess,
we're too jittery to travel after Michael's death."
You are still magisterial and cocky as when
you gave us young romantics our directive,
"Shoot when you get the chance, only shoot to kill."
Who else would sire twin sons at sixty-eight?
How sweet your life in retirement! What better than loving
a young wife and boy; without curses writing,
"I shall not live long enough to 'see him through.'"

Three Poems *1.* *Seal of the Fair Sex*

"He was mother's beau before she spoke to boys—
our *Uncle* Harold. Now his eyes are going,
he pops in here twice a week with Maine delights,
his colorful, slightly aging garden truck,
his bounty to needy and unneedy since we knew him. . . .
Thirty raspberry bushes stacked on my sundeck,
then planted and meshed by himself in three small rows,
with three plastic lilies, his everlastings,
just like a grave—*for you to think of me,
when I lie uphill.* Do you find this amusing?
He is in love, I am the end-all crush.
When we are gone and dying, love is power,
love, in his hallucinated sunrise, keeps him . . .
it's all that kept off death at any time."

Three Poems 2. River Harbor

I sit desiring a more historic harbor,
wilds suiting our first Academy's pomp of youth,
or Aaron Burr's flirtation with frontiers—
we swing with our warpage to *fin de siècle*—
down river, down river, and none will go to town. . . .
Your wharfpiles leaking sawdust ran half a mile—
rot without burden. Your shack was a cookie-box,
your costly small motors moved electric-sculptures,
toys for the lover of Klee. Art for you was amusement,
child drowning the summer in puzzles and shady tennis. . . .
We lay under glass of a greenhouse at noon,
all visible for a fling of fifty miles,
North Haven, Stonington and Mount Desert—
your toy structures flecking in my eyes like flies.

Three Poems 3. Shipwreck Party

One misses Emerson drowned in Luminism,
his vast serenity of emptiness;
and FitzHugh Lane painting a schooner moored in Castine,
its bright flywings fixed in the topographical
severity of a world reworked as glass.
Tools are honest function, and even toys;
you puzzled out small devices, mini-motors,
set children and parents trotting in your trash,
you danced dressed as a beercan, crosscut, zany thing—
wit and too much contrivance for our yacht club brawl.
After the party, I heard your unmuffled car
loop the town, ten or twelve laps a minute—
a village is too small to lose a date
or need a hatchet to split hairs.

Hudson River Dream

I like trees, because I can never be at their eye-level;
not even when the stiff sash of the snowed-in farmhouse
slammed, as it always did, toward morning-rise;
I dreaming I was sailing a very small sailboat,
with my mother one-eighth Jewish, and *her* mother two-eighths,
down the Hudson, twice as wide as it is, wide as the Mississippi,
sliding under the pylons of the George Washington Bridge,
lacework groins as tall as twenty trees
(childhood's twice-as-wide and twice-as-high),
docking through the coalsmoke at a river café.
The Atlantic draws the river to no end. . . .
My knee-joints melted when I met you—
O why was I born of woman? Never to reach their eye-level,
seeing women's mouths while my date delays in the john.

Blood Test, 1931, after about forty Years

Boarding, not bedding, at the Haven Inn,
I fourteen and just not missing breakfast
to catch you alone with coffee and stacked plates—
I dared not smile, so you didn't. You were eighteen,
you had been about, and were. . . .
Do the sheep your mother rented still mow the lawn
they dirty? Is her ruddy decollatage of just-forty . . .
She died that winter. . . . I watched you with my head half off—
all, all, the mind, the bones, the flesh, the soul . . .
gone in the peripheral flotsam of our live flow?
I see my blood pumped into crystal pipes,
little sticks like the firecrackers of live July—
ninetenths of me water, yet it's lousy stuff—
touch blood, it sticks, stains, drips, slides . . . and it's lukewarm.

Last Resort

The sunrise, the *cri de coeur*, my swat at age—
everyone now is crowding everyone
to stretch vacation until Indian Summer. . . .
Old People in thirty canebacks view Vermont,
a golf course, and the everlasting hills.
This club is open to all who worship health—
in quantity or inns, we terrify,
asking to linger on past fall in Eden.
Cold cracks the supple golf-shoe; we warm our cars,
burn the thruway to Boston and the world. . . . *Age*:
an old house sunk and glum, a smell of turtles,
my grandparents' bridal portrait fades to carbon—
youth that gave no youth, an old world marriage.
Didn't she love him when she loved his clothes?

Dream of Fair Ladies

Those maidens' high waists, languid steel and wedding cake,
fell, as waists must, and the white, white bust, to heel—
these once, the new wave; mostly they were many,
and would not let the children speak. They spoke
making a virtue of lost innocence.
They were never sober after ten
because life hit them, as it must by forty;
whenever they smoothed a dead cheek, it bled.
High-waisted maidens, languid steel and wedding cake . . .
they lost us on the road from chapel to graveyard.
Pace, pace, they asked for no man's seeding. . . .
Meeting them here is like ten years back home,
when hurting others was as necessary as breathing,
hurting myself more necessary than breathing.

Randall Jarrell *1. October 1965*

Sixty, seventy, eighty: I would see you mellow,
unchanging grasshopper, whistling down the grass-fires;
the same hair, snow-touched, and wrist for tennis; soon double
not singles. . . . Who dares go with you to your deadfall,
see the years wrinkling up the reservoir,
watch the ivy turning a wash of blood
on your infirmary wall? Thirty years ago,
as students waiting for Europe and spring term to end—
we saw below us, golden, small, stockstill,
the college polo field, cornfields, the feudal airdrome,
the McKinley Trust; behind, above us, the tower,
the dorms, the fieldhouse, the Bishop's palace and chapel—
Randall, the scene still plunges at the windshield,
apples redden to ripeness on the whiplash bough.

Randall Jarrell *2*

I grizzle the embers of our onetime life,
our first intoxicating disenchantments,
dipping our hands once, not twice in the newness . . .
coming back to Kenyon on the Ohio local—
the view, middle distance, back and foreground, shifts,
silos shifting squares like chessmen—a wheel
turned by the water buffalo through the blue
of true space before the dawn of days. . . .
Then the night of the caged squirrel on his wheel,
lights, eyes, peering at you from the overpass;
black-gloved, black-coated, you plod out stubbornly
as if in lockstep to grasp your blank not-I
at the foot of the tunnel . . . as if asleep, Child Randall,
greeting the cars, and approving—your harsh luminosity.

126

Munich 1938, John Crowe Ransom

Hitler, Mussolini, Daladier, Chamberlain,
that historic confrontation of the great—
voluble on one thing, they hated war—
each lost there pushing the war ahead twelve months.
Was it worse to choke on the puke of prudence,
or blow up Europe for a point of honor? . . .
John Crowe Ransom, Kenyon College, Gambier, Ohio,
looking at primitive African art on loan:
gleam-bottomed warriors of oiled brown wood,
waving broom-straws in their hands for spears;
far from the bearded, bronze ur-Nordic hoplites
of Athens and Sparta, not distant from their gods.
John said, "Well, they may not have been good neighbors,
but they haven't troubled the rest of the world."

Picture in The Literary Life, a Scrapbook

A mag photo, before I was I, or my books—
a listener. . . . A cheekbone gumballs out my cheek;
too much live hair. My wife caught in that eye blazes,
an egg would boil in the tension of that hand,
my untied shoestrings write my name in the dust. . . .
I lean against the tree, and sharpen bromides
to serve our great taskmaster, the New Critic,
who loved the writing better than we ourselves. . . .
In those days, if I pressed an ear to the earth,
I heard the bass growl of Hiroshima.
In the *Scrapbook*, it's only the old die classics:
one foot in the grave, two fingers in their Life.
Who would rather be his indexed correspondents
than the boy Keats spitting out blood for time to breathe?

Frederick Kuh, Manx Cat

(FOR JEAN STAFFORD)

Closer to us than most of our close friends,
the only friend we never quarrelled over,
the sole survivor of our first marriage, I see him
on catnip, bobtailed, bobbing like a rabbit,
streaking up the slender wand of a tree,
scratching the polished bark and glassy sprouts,
preferring to hang hooked than lift a claw.
Windtoy, Lynxears, Furfall, you had eyes,
you lowered yourself to us, clockclaw, clickclaw—
to where no one backed down or lost a point.
Cats aren't quite lost despite too many lives.
Which of us will ever manage one,
or storm the heights and gracefully back down—
Jean, those years multiplied beyond subtraction?

Family Album

Those mute dinner parties, wife by husband,
no passenger having seniority over father,
rank won at the captain's table first day at sea—
INDISPENSABLE . . . like Franklin Roosevelt,
dying and solar on his fourth campaign—
coming to power by reaching public opinion—
the sad blandness of the silver voice;
he used time, time was his servant not his master . . . .
You learn to be yourself; at first it's freedom,
then paralysis, since you are yourself. . . .
Free in the teeth of the world's first army,
they snatched their third of a million men from Dunkirk;
for the first time England was spiritually in the war,
the defeat, like so many British retreats, a triumph.

128

Deutschland über Alles

Hitler, though we laughed, gave them the start,
the step forward, one had to give them that:
the Duce's, "Once they start marching, they'll never stop—"
the silver reichsmark sticking to the heel,
the knights corrupted by their purity,
made wilder by the wildness of the woodcut—
his eyes were glowing coals, a world gone dark,
the horde, on stopwatch, asked for earth and water,
settled for *lebensraum*, then *lebensraum*:
spaces, a space, the knight astride the eyetooth,
joy in the introversion of loneliness.
Who will contest the conqueror his dirt,
spaces enough to bury what he left,
the six million Jews gassed in the space to breathe?

In the Cage

(FIRST WRITTEN 1944)

We short-termers file into the messhall
according to our houses—twos
of bleaching denim. A felon fairy
tinkles dinner-music blues,
blows kisses from his balustrade;
a canary chips its bars and screams.
We come from the prison cellar . . . spade,
pickax, hod for plaster, steam,
asbestos. To the anti-semite
black Bible-garbling Israelite
starving on wheatseeds for religion,
I am night, I am vanity. The cage
feeds our failed nerve for service.
Fear, the yellow chirper, beaks its cage.

Rats

That friend of the war years, the Israelite
on my masons' gang at our model jail,
held his hand over the postcard Connecticut
landscape, pocked by prisoners and a few safe human
houses, *Only man is miserable.*
He was wrong though, he forgot the rats. A pair
in an enclosure kills the rest, then breeds a clan.
Stranger rats with their wrong clan-smell stumble
on the clan, are run squeaking with tails and backs split open
up trees and fences—they die of nervous shock.
Someone rigged the enclosure with electric levers
that could give the rats orgasms. Soon they learned
to press the levers, did nothing else—still on the trip,
they died of starvation in a litter of food.

Hell

"Nth Circle of Dante—and in the dirt-roofed cave,
each family had marked off its yard of space;
no light except for coal fires laid in buckets,
no draft of air except the reek, no water,
no hole to hide the excrement. I walked,
afraid of stumbling on the helpless bodies,
afraid of going in circles. I lost the Fascist
or German deserters I was hunting . . . screaming
vecchi, women, children, coughing and cursing.
Then hit my foot on someone and reached out
to keep from falling or hurting anyone;
and what I touched was not the filthy floor:
a woman's hand returning my worried grasp,
her finger tracing my lifeline on my palm."

Streamers: 1970

The London windows bloomed with Christmas streamers
twenty-five days before their Christmas Day
I will not see if I can reach New York;
but I was divorced from my passport—
"The Home Office can't keep your passport, it isn't theirs,
it isn't yours even, it's God's, or Nixon's."
Everything gets lost in life's strip-tease—
who stripped for the guards at Auschwitz? They caught whores
good Germans, and married them themselves for Hitler—
one assumes those marriages were consummated;
who'd marry a whore to read *Mein Kampf* in bed?
After the weddings they packed the wives in planes;
altitude gained, the girls were pushed outdoors—
their parachutes their streaming bridal veils.

Serpent

"When I was changed from a feeble cosmopolite
to a fanatical antisemite,
I didn't let you chew my time with chatter,
bury my one day's reasonable explanations
in your equal verisimilitude the next. . . .
But I got to the schools, their hysterical faith
in the spoken word, hypnotic hammer blows,
indelible, ineradicable,
the politician wedded to a mind—
I come once in a blue moon.. . . I my age
its magical interpretation of the world,
enslaved to will and not intelligence. . . .
Soon it was obvious I didn't enjoy my war.
I'd no time for concerts, theater, to go to movies."

Words

Christ's first portrait was a donkey's head,
the simple truth is in his simple word,
lies buried in a random, haggard sentence,
cutting ten ways to nothing clearly carried. . . .
In our time, God is an entirely lost person—
there were two: Benito Mussolini and Hitler,
blind mouths shouting people into things.
After their Chicago deaths with girls and Lügers,
we know they gave a plot to what they planned.
No league against the ephemeral Enemy lasts;
not even the aristocracy of the Commune
curing the seven plagues of economics,
to wither daily in favor of the state,
a covenant of swords without the word.

Sunrise

There is always enough daylight in hell to blind;
the flower of what was left grew sweeter for them,
two done people conversing with bamboo fans
as if to brush the firefall from the air—
Admiral Onishi, still a cult to his juniors,
the father of the Kamikazes . . . he became a fish-hawk
flying our armadas down like game;
his young pilots loved him to annihilation.
He chats in his garden, the sky is zigzag fire.
One butchery is left, his wife keeps nagging him to do it.
Husband and wife taste cup after cup of Scotch;
how garrulously they patter about their grandchildren—
when his knife goes home, it goes home wrong. . . .
For eighteen hours you died with your hand in hers.

In the Forties *1*

'46 and greenwood sizzling on the andirons,
two men of iron, two milk-faced British Redcoats.
June smoulders to greenness; in the sopping trees
the greenfrog whistles to the baser shush
of new leaves; thrush and robin go a-hunting,
heads cocked for earthworms sunning in the thaws. . . .
Friends came, new as the foliage of the season;
you came, unique in making me take walks.
One day we discovered—or did we—mounds
of the Abenaki, R.C. converts like me;
some humorist called them Praying Niggers, though
this helped them little with the English, who
scalped, killed and burned brave, squaw and child—then held
that field a moment . . . as we, newcomers, free.

In the Forties *2*

The heron warps its neck, a broken pick,
to study its reflection in the glare
of the lily pads bright as mica, swarming
with plant-lice in the wood-red water.
I see you: your ballet glasses hold
the heron twisting by a fist of alder,
your figure's synonym—your chest so thin then,
the ribs stood out like bars. . . . The Puritan shone here,
lord of self-inflicted desiccation,
roaming for outlet through the virgin forest,
stalking the less mechanically angered savage—
the warpath to three wives and twenty children—
many of them, too many, Love, to count,
born like us to fill graveyards . . . thick as sticks.

By August, Brooklyn turned autumn, all
Prospect Pond could mirror. No sound; no talk;
dead matches nicked the water and expired
in target-circles of inverted sky,
nature's looking-glass . . . a little cold!
Our day was cold and short, love, and its sun
numb as the red carp, twenty inches long,
panting, a weak old dog, below a smashed
oar floating from the musty dock. . . . The fish
is fungus now; I wear a swollen face. . . .
I rowed for our reflection, but it slid
between my hands aground. There the squirrel,
a conservative and vegetarian,
keeps his roots and freehold, Love, unsliding.

F. O. Matthiessen 1902–50

Matthiessen jumping from the North Boston hotel,
breaking his mania barrier to despair;
a patriot like the Czech-student human torches?
Or manslaughter? Who knows whom he might have killed,
falling bald there like a shell. I'm scared
of hitting this street, his street so far to our left
in gala anti-Stalinist 1950—
I wouldn't murder and be murdered for my soul,
like Stonewall Jackson sucking the soul of a lemon. . . .
Mattie, his Yale *Skull and Bones* pin on the dresser,
torn between the homosexual's terrible love
for forms, and his anarchic love of man . . .
died, unique as the Union, lies frozen meat,
fast colors lost to lust and prosecution.

Sylvia Plath

A miniature mad talent? Sylvia Plath,
who'll wipe off the spit of your integrity,
rising in the saddle to slash at Auschwitz,
life tearing this or that, *I am a woman*?
Who'll lay the graduate girl in marriage,
queen bee, naked, unqueenly, shaming her shame?
Each English major saying, "*I* am Sylvia,
I hate marriage, I must hate babies."
Even men have a horror of giving birth,
mother-sized babies splitting us in half,
sixty thousand American infants a year,
U.I.D., Unexplained Infant Deaths,
born physically whole and hearty, refuse to live,
Sylvia . . . the expanding torrent of your attack.

Randall Jarrell

The dream went like a rake of sliced bamboo,
slats of dust distracted by a downdraw;
I woke and knew I held a cigarette;
I looked, there was none, could have been none;
I slept off years before I woke again,
palming the floor, shaking the sheets. I saw
nothing was burning. I awoke, I saw
I was holding two lighted cigarettes. . . .
They come this path, old friends, old buffs of death.
Tonight it's Randall, his spark still fire though humble,
his gnawed wrist cradled like *Kitten*. "What kept you so long,
racing the cooling grindstone of your ambition?
You didn't write, you *re*wrote. . . . But tell me,
Cal, why did we live? Why do we die?"

Theodore Roethke 1908–63

At Yaddo, you shared a bathroom with a bag
tree-painter whose boobs bounced in the basin,
your blues basin where you wished to plunge your head. . . .
All night, my friend, no friend, you swam in my sleep;
this morning you are lost in the Maine sky,
close, cold, gray, smoke and smoke-colored cloud.
Sheeplike, unsociable, reptilian, the shags
fly off in lines like duck in a shooting booth,
divers devolving to a monochrome.
You honored nature, helpless, elemental
creature, and touched the waters of the offing;
you left them quickened with your name: Ted Roethke. . . .
Omnipresent, the Mother made you nonexistent,
you, the ocean's anchor and high out-tide.

In Dreams begin Responsibilities

My heater aches my head, it's cold outside,
it's bright outside, the sun tears stars in my shade . . .
the problem is to keep the dream a movie:
a hundred breasts are bursting the same black sweater,
like and unlike as the stars or the snowflakes.
Your dream had humor, then its genius thickened,
you grew thick and helpless, your lines were variants,
unlike and alike, Delmore—your name, Schwartz,
one vowel bedevilled by seven consonants . . .
one gabardine suit the color of sulphur,
scanning wide-eyed the windowless room of wisdom,
your notes on Joyce and porno magazines—
the stoplights blinking code for you alone
casing the bars with the eye of a Mongol horseman.

136

Tabletalk with Names 1970

"Why don't you write the things he should have written:
Nelson Rockefeller letching for his wife,
Delmore even hallucinating the room. . . ."
The boy wearing his black fleece mini-coat to lunch,
lace ragging his freshly laundered shirt,
his cufflinks sterling silver bottletops,
his longhand verses published in holograph.
"London is less terrible than New York,
but I will never storm the citadel."
He equally enjoyed the notables he taped:
Elsa Morante, Ezra, his Senator's wife.
"One of my lovely ladies." I must hold the table,
snapping at his questions like a queen,
another master's voice to fill the album.

Our Dead Poets

Their lines string out from nowhere, stretch to sorrow.
I think of the others who once had the top billing,
ironclads in our literary havoc,
now even forgotten by malice. "He exists,"
as an old Stalinist luminary said of a friend
sent to Siberia, "Cold helps him to compose."
As a child Jean Stafford stood on a chair to dress;
"It's so much easier." It's easier not to dress,
not brush our teeth, flick off unopened mail.
Sometimes for days I only hear your voices,
the sun of summer will not adorn you again
with her garment of new leaves and flowers . . .
her *nostalgie de la boue* that shelters ape
and protozoa from the rights of man.

137

For Ann Adden 1. 1958

Remember standing with me in the dark,
Ann Adden? In the mad house? Everything—
I mad, you mad for me? And brought my ring,
that twelve-carat lunk of gold there . . . Joan of Arc . . .
undeviating still from your true mark—
robust, ah taciturn! Remember our playing
Marian Anderson in Mozart's *Shepherd King*,
Il Re Pastore there? O Hammerheaded Shark,
the Rainbow Salmon of the World, your hand
a rose—not there, a week earlier! We stand,
sky-walking the eggshell by the Mittersill,
Pascal's infinite, perfect, fearful sphere—
the border nowhere, your center everywhere. . . .
And if I forget you, Ann, may my right hand . . .

For Ann Adden 2. Heidegger Student

"Have you ever lost a year off . . . somewhere?
The new owner can't give it back to us, can he?
Our terrible losses, but Harry Truman couldn't
lose a minute's sleep for Hiroshima—
a boy who slammed the paw of his mutt in the door of his
        car would. . . .
Twice I heard a rattling stress of cherry-stones,
saw from my bed, the man. My flight was Gothic
with steel-gloved hand, shoe filled with blood, and wings. . . .
And I killed my dragon—my doctor's thesis on Heidegger
in Germany, in German, for my German Prof.
I love Lenin, he was so feudal. *When I listen to Beethoven,*
he said, *I think of stroking people's hair;*
what we need are people to chop the head off.
The horizontal is the color of blood . . ."

138

For *Ann Adden 3. 1968*

"Dear Lowell, sitting sixty feet above the sea,
hearing my father build our house on this cliff,
sixty feet above the Penobscot Bay,
returning here from ten years exile in Europe,
waiting for our emigration papers, work cards . . .
I chanced to read your Adden poem in *Near the Ocean.*
You're older . . . an extending potency. . . .
What I'd like to say is humanity,
as if a cubist lept to pharaohs in blackstone.
What I write to tell you is what a shining
remembrance for someone, you, to hold of me—
we aggrandize 1958,
the snow-capped, crazy, virginal year, I fled
America. We have a Viking son of three."

For *Anne Adden 4. Coda*

I want you to see me when I have one head
again, not many, like a bunch of grapes.
The universe moves beneath me when I move,
a stream of heady, terrified poured stone. . . .
On my great days of sickness, I was God—
cry of blood for high blood that gives both tyrant
and tyrannized their short half-holiday. . . .
Now the earth is solid, the sky is light,
yet even on the steadiest day, dead noon,
I have to brace my hand against a wall
to keep myself from swaying—swaying wall,
straitjacket, hypodermic, helmeted
doctors, one crowd, white-smocked, in panic, hit,
and bury me running on the cleated field.

139

T. S. Eliot

Caught between two streams of traffic, in the gloom
of Memorial Hall and Harvard's war-dead. . . . And he:
"Don't you loathe to be compared with your relatives?
I do. I've just found two of mine reviewed by Poe.
He wiped the floor with them . . . and I was *delighted*."
Then on with warden's pace across the Yard,
talking of Pound, "It's balls to say he only
pretends to be Ezra. . . . He's better though. This year,
he no longer wants to rebuild the Temple at Jerusalem.
Yes, he's better. '*You* speak,' he said, when he'd talked two hours.
By then I had absolutely nothing to *say*."
Ah Tom, one muse, one music, had one your luck—
lost in the dark night of the brilliant talkers,
humor and honor from the everlasting dross!

Ezra Pound

Horizontal on a deckchair in the ward
of the criminal mad. . . . A man without shoestrings clawing
the Social Credit broadside from your table, you saying,
". . . here with a black suit and black briefcase; in the brief,
an abomination, Possum's *hommage* to Milton."
Then sprung; Rapallo, and the decade gone;
and three years later, Eliot dead, you saying,
"Who's left alive to understand my jokes?
My old Brother in the arts . . . besides, he was a smash of a
     poet."
You showed me your blotched, bent hands, saying, "Worms.
When I talked that nonsense about Jews on the Rome
wireless, Olga knew it was shit, and still loved me."
And I, "Who else has been in Purgatory?"
You, "I began with a swelled head and end with swelled feet."
140

Fears of Going Blind

(FOR WYNDHAM LEWIS)

El Greco could paint a thunderstorm reflected
on a cufflink; Americans reflect
the space they peopled. . . . I see non sequitur:
Watch the stoplights, they are leopards' eyes;
what's the word for God, if he has four legs? . . .
Even the artist's vision picks up dirt,
the jelly behind the eyeball will leak out,
you will live with constellations of flusters,
comet-flashes from the outer corners;
see the failed surgeon exit with a smile,
they will not let you move your head for weeks,
your wife will hold up gin in a teacup to your mouth,
you will suck from a crooked straw—what depresses
me is they'll actually take my eyeball out.

Louis MacNeice 1907–63

A dozen children would visit half a dozen;
downstairs a lost child bullied the piano,
getting from note to note was jumping railties;
the black keys showed bruises and turned white.
The outdoor games the child heard outside and missed
were as heavily hit and commonplace—
no need to be Bach to be what we are. . . .
Louis, watching his father, the Bishop, wade
a trout-stream barefoot, watching for the first time liked him:
"What poor feet!" Till thirty, he was afraid
a trout-stream barefoot, for the first time liked him:
A month from his death, we talked by Epstein's bust
of Eliot; MacNeice said, "It is better
to die at fifty than lose our pleasure in fear."

William Carlos Williams

Who loved more? William Carlos Williams,
in collegiate black slacks, gabardine coat,
and loafers polished like rosewood on yachts,
straying stonefoot through his town-end garden,
man and flower seedy with three autumn strokes,
his brown, horned eyes enlarged, an ant's, through glasses;
his Mother, stonedeaf, her face a wizened talon,
her hair the burnt-out ash of lush Puerto Rican grass;
her black, blind, bituminous eye inquisitorial.
"Mama," he says, "which would you rather see here,
me or two blondes?" Then later, "The old bitch
is over a hundred, I'll kick off tomorrow."
He said, "I am sixty-seven, and more
attractive to girls than when I was seventeen."

Robert Frost

Robert Frost at midnight, the audience gone
to vapor, the great act laid on the shelf in mothballs,
his voice is musical and raw—he writes in the flyleaf:
For Robert from Robert, his friend in the art.
"Sometimes I feel too full of myself," I say.
And he, misunderstanding, "When I am low,
I stray away. My son wasn't your kind. The night
we told him Merrill Moore would come to treat him,
he said, 'I'll kill him first.' One of my daughters thought things,
thought every male she met was out to make her;
the way she dressed, she couldn't make a whorehouse."
And I, "Sometimes I'm so happy I can't stand myself."
And he, "When I am too full of joy, I think
how little good my health did anyone near me."

142

Stalin

Winds on the stems make them creak like manmade things;
a hedge of vines and bushes—three or four
kinds, grape-leaf, elephant-ear and alder,
an arabesque, imperfect and alive,
a hundred hues of green, the darkest shades
fall short of black, the whitest leaf-back short of white.
The state, if we could see behind the wall,
is woven of perishable vegetation.
Stalin? What shot him clawing up the tree of power—
millions plowed under with the crops they grew,
his intimates dying like the spider-bridegroom?
The large stomach could only chew success. What raised him
was an unusual lust to break the icon,
joke cruelly, seriously, and be himself.

Harpo Marx

Harpo Marx, your hands white-feathered the harp—
the only words you ever spoke were sound.
The movie's not always the sick man of the arts,
yours touched the stars; Harpo, your motion picture
is still life unchanging, not nature dead.
You dumbly memorized an unwritten script. . . .
I saw you first two years before you died,
a black-and-white fall, near Fifth in Central Park:
old blond hair too blonder, old eyes too young.
Movie trucks and five police trucks wheel to wheel
like covered wagons. The crowd as much or little.
I wish I had knelt. . . . I age to your wincing smile,
like Dante's movie, the great glistening wheel of life—
the genius *happy* . . . a generic actor.

The Goldfish

The biggest cat sees all through eyefilm, yawns
dreamily, "Such a sweet little radical couple!"
And prays for the man to come without his wife.
Her decks of windows graze on Central Park,
her fortune flies from Zurich to meet the rent—
from her elevation the crowd is part of a movie.
"Is it as Marx dreamed, man is what he makes?"
She sees the Old Left yielding place to New,
the unilluminating city lights,
as a goldfish might calculate the universe.
She sees the Old Left yielding place to New,
and eyes her guest, young, dissident, a trustee;
tonight he is single, he has everything,
swims in her like an eel in the Bay of Fundy.

Across Central Park

Home from you, and through the trodden tangle,
the corny birdwalk, the pubescent knoll,
rowboats three deep on the landing, tundra
from Eighty-First Street to my 15 Sixty-Seventh,
snow going from pepper and salt to brain-cell dull,
winter throwing off its Christmas decorations.
The afternoon has darkened in twenty minutes
from light to night—I think of seeing you
in General Eisenhower's Washington,
I in a Dickensian muffler, snow-sugared, unraveling. . . .
You've lived the season. In the waste loss
of revelations, your true voice has seared,
still yearningly young; and I, though never young
since our first meeting, am younger when we meet.

Che Guevara
(CENTRAL PARK)
Week of Che Guevara, hunted, hurt,
held prisoner one lost day, then gangstered down
for gold, for justice—violence cracking on violence,
rock on rock, the corpse of our last armed prophet
laid out on a sink in a shed, revealed by flashlight. . . .
The leaves light up, still green, this afternoon,
and burn to frittered reds; our tree, branch-lopped
to go on living, swells with homely goiters—
under uniform sixteen story Park apartments . . .
the poor Latins much too new for our new world,
Manhattan where our clasped, illicit hands
pulse, stop my bloodstream as if I'd hit rock. . . .
Rest for the outlaw . . . kings once hid in trees
with prices on their heads, and watched for game.

Caracas 1

Through another of our cities without a center,
Los Angeles, and with as many cars
per foot, and past the 20-foot neon sign
for *Coppertone* on the cathedral, past the envied,
$700 per capita a year
in jerry skyscraper living slabs—to the White House
of El Presidente Leoni, his small men with 18-
inch repeating pistols, firing 45 bullets a minute,
two armed guards frozen beside us, and our champagne . . .
someone bugging the President: "Where are the girls?"
And the enclosed leader, quite a fellow, saying,
"I don't know where yours are, I know where to find mine". . . .
This house, this pioneer democracy, built
on foundations, not of rock, but blood as hard as rock.

Caracas 2

If words were handled like the new grass rippling,
far from planners, the vile writhings of our nerves . . .
One could get through life, though mute, with courage
and a merciful heart—two things, and the first thing:
humor . . . as the evicted squatter clings
with amused bravery that takes the form of mercy
to the Old Caracas Square—its shaky, one-man hovels,
its cathedral first spoiled in the age of Drake.
The church has hay in its courtyard; the hovel owns the Common—
no grass as green as the greens in the open sewer . . .
conservatives reduced to conservation:
communists committed to their commune—
artists and office-holders to a claque
of less than fifty . . . to each his venomous in-group.

Norman Mailer

The 9 a.m. man on the street is a new
phenomenon to me: he moves. He moves
in one direction for Fifth Avenue,
and up Fifth Avenue, simplex as pigeons,
as crocked with project, his heart, a watch,
imagining being paid for being on time. . . .
In Buenos Aires, the bourgeois is the clock,
his heart on Greenwich, the West's last Anglophile,
his constitutionals a reek of tweed—
being erratic isn't the only way
to be ourselves, or Norman Mailer—he wears
a wardrobe of two identical straight blue suits
and two blue vests . . . to prove monotony,
escape the many false faces I see as one.

Liberty and Revolution, Buenos Aires

At the *Hotel Continental* I always
heard the bulky, beefy, breathing herd.
I had bought a cow suit and matching chestnut
flatter pointed shoes that hurt my toes.
That day cast the light of the next world: the bellow
of Juan Peron, the schoolgirls' Don Giovanni—
frowning starch-collared crowds, a *coup d'état*—
I missed it—of the leaden internecine soldier,
the lump of dough on the chessboard. . . . By darkening cypress,
the Republican martyrs lie in Roman temples;
marble goddesses calm each Liberal hero
still pale from the great kiss of Liberty. . . .
All night till my shoes were bloody—I found rest
cupping my soft palm to her stone breast.

Statue of Liberty

I like you like trees . . . you make me lift my eyes—
the treasonable bulge behind your iron toga,
the thrilling, chilling silver of your laugh,
the hysterical digging of your accursed spur,
Amazon, gazing on me, pop-eyed, cool,
ageless, not holding back your war-whoop—no chicken,
still game for swimming bare-ass with the boys.
You catch the frenetic spotlight we sling about
your lighthouse promontory, flights an inch
from combustion and the drab of ash. . . .
While youth lasts your flesh is never fallen—
high above our perishable flesh,
the icy foamrubber waterfall stands firm
metal, pear-pointing to eternity.

147

Can a plucked Bird Live?

From the first cave, the first farm, the first sage,
inalienable the human right to kill—
"You must get used," they say, "to seeing guns,
to using guns." Guns too are mortal. Guns
failed Che Guevara, Marie Antoinette,
Leon Trotsky, the children of the Tsar—
chivalrous ornaments to power. Tom Paine said
Burke pitied the plumage and forgot the dying bird.
Arms given the people are always used against the people—
a dolphin of spirit poking up its snout
into the red steam of that limitless daybreak
would breathe the intoxication of Rimbaud. . . .
Are there guns that will not kill the possessor?
Our raised hands—fear made wise by anger.

The March *1*

(FOR DWIGHT MACDONALD)
Under the too white marmoreal Lincoln Memorial,
the too tall marmoreal Washington Obelisk,
gazing into the too long reflecting pool,
the reddish trees, the withering autumn sky,
the remorseless, amplified harangues for peace—
lovely to lock arms, to march absurdly locked
(unlocking to keep my wet glasses from slipping)
to see the cigarette match quaking in my fingers,
then to step off like green Union Army recruits
for the first Bull Run, sped by photographers,
the notables, the girls . . . fear, glory, chaos, rout . . .
our green army staggered out on the miles-long green fields,
met by the other army, the Martian, the ape, the hero,
his new-fangled rifle, his green new steel helmet.

The March 2

Where two or three were flung together, or fifty,
mostly white-haired, or bald, or women . . . sadly
unfit to follow their dream, I sat in the sunset
shade of our Bastille, the Pentagon,
nursing leg- and arch-cramps, my cowardly,
foolhardy heart; and heard, alas, more speeches,
though the words took heart now to show how weak
we were, and right. An MP sergeant kept
repeating, "March slowly through them. Don't even brush
anyone sitting down." They tiptoed through us
in single file, and then their second wave
trampled us flat and back. Health to those who held,
health to the green steel head . . . to your kind hands
that helped me stagger to my feet, and flee.

Pacification of Columbia

Great dome, small domes or turbans, a child's blue sky,
exhalations of the desert sand—
my old jigsawpuzzle Mosque of Mecca
flung to vaultless consummation and consumed
by Allah—but the puzzle had no message. . . .
The destructive element emaciates
Columbia this Mayday afternoon;
the thickened buildings look like painted buildings,
Raphael's colossal classic sags on the canvas.
Horses, higher artistic types than their masters,
forage Broadway's median trees, as if
nature were liberation . . . the blue police
chew soundlessly by the burnished, nervous hides,
as if they'd learned to meet together in reason.

The Restoration

The old king enters his study with the police;
it's much like mine left in my hands a month:
unopened letters, the thousand dead cigarettes,
open books, yogurt cups in the unmade bed—
the old king enters his study with the police,
but all in all his study is much worse than mine;
an edge of malice shows the thumb of man:
frames smashed, their honorary honours lost,
all his unopened letters have been answered.
He halts at woman-things that can't be his,
and says, "To think that human beings did this!"
The sergeant picks up a defiled *White Goddess*,
or the old king's offprints on ideograms,
"Would a human beings do this things to these book?"

Leader of the Left

Though justice ascribe it to his blind ambition,
and blinder courage (both sowed their dirty germs)
not some ostracizing glandular imbalance—
the miracle of poverty opened his eyes;
his whole face took on a flesh of wood,
a slab of raw plastic grafted to his one
natural feature, scars from demonstrations
borne like a Heidelberg student for the New Left. . . .
His voice, electric, only burns low current;
by now he's bypassed sense and even eloquence—
without listening, his audience believe;
anticipating his sentence, they accept
the predestined poignance of his murder,
his Machiavellian Utopia of pure nerve.

The New York Intellectual

How often was his last paragraph recast?
Did Irving really want three hundred words,
such tact and tough, ascetic resonance,
the preposition *for*, five times in parallel,
to find himself "a beleaguered minority,
without fantasies of martyrdom,"
facing the graves of the New York Intellectuals,
"without joy, but neither with dismay"?
(Art was needed for this final sentence.)
Others read the obsequies with dismay.
What gifts or weakness changed the sick provincial
out-of-it West Side intellectual
to the great brazen rhetorician serpent,
swimming the current with his iron smile?

Historian's Daughter

"Yachts still out, though the saltmarsh is frost;
back for the funeral in my old town, New London,
I know the names of people not their faces.
What did I do to myself? I painted, often
using my hand for a brush. I could be someone,
though only a model, if I photographed.
My peer-group, students, graduates, hippies, mean less
to me than the wasp dropouts of sixty in bars.
But Father believed we needed a bracing man
like Harry Truman—Father was a bang
to do Japan with: he was never stoned,
never irrelevant; at each new airport,
he did five postcards, or recorded history—
our background had no grace for using sloth."

Worse Times

In college, we harangued our platitudes,
and hit democracy with Plato's corkscrew—
we demanded art as disciplined
and dark as Marx or Calvin's *Institutes*—
there was precedent for this argument:
flames from the open hearth of Thor and Saul,
beef frescoed on the vaults of cave and clan,
fleshpots, firewater, slung chunks of awk and man—
the missiles no dialectician's hand could turn.
Children have called the anthropoid, father;
he'd stay home Sunday, and they walked on coals. . . .
The passage from lower to upper middle age
is quicker than the sigh of a match in the water—
we too were students, and betrayed our hand.

Student

France died on the motionless lines of Marshal Joffre. . . .
We have found new saints and Roundhead cells
to guide us down the narrow path and hard,
standing on stilts to curse their black-ice heaven—
Marshal Stalin was something of an artist
at this vague, dreamlike trade of blood and guile—
his joke was death—meat stuck between his tooth
and gum began to stink in half a second.
If I could stop growing, I would stop at twenty,
free to be ill-at-ease again as everyone,
go a-whoring, a-kneeling before the masters,
wallpapering my unlocked cell with paper classics. . . .
Love at fifty is outdrinking the siren;
she sings the Kill-river of no cure.

Small College Riot

The bonfire is eating the green uprooted trees
and bakes cracks in the slabs of the Sixties piazza:
half-moon of students, coughing disk-hymns to pot;
the firemen leave a sizzle of black ink—
a second fire blazes in the facing corner.
On a glassed-in corridor, we professors—
fans of the Colosseum—wipe our glasses
primed for the gladiatorial matinee—
but won't someone move? The students move the firemen;
a boy in a wheelchair burns his lecture-notes,
and hangs his clothes to dry on the green fume—
naked . . . no shorts. Our guest speaker on Shelley
says, "If I met a student, I might have to kill him."
Four legendary oiltanks—are they under the fire?

Professor of Tenure

Wars have silenced half the classic tongues. . . .
The professor holds the chair of tenure,
ink licked from the warts and creases of his skin,
vapor of venom, commonplace and joy—
whenever he croaks, a rival has to plunge,
his girl with a taperecorder has total recall,
his students scribble—*Of course we have the bombs;*
what's wanting is the nerve to play the music,
smash East Germany and Poland in two days,
burn Russia with our nuclear typhoon,
blast Cairo, Damascus, China back to sand.
This Machiavel is one the world can buy;
he's held us to the rough these twenty years,
unchanging since he found no salad in change. . . .

The Spock Sentences in Boston

The black hardrubber bathtub stoppers at the Parker House
must have been ordered for their Majesties,
Edward VII and Queen Alexandra,
the weight and pull of William Howard Taft.
Things were made right in those days—18-carat
gold sky over Boston, brass beds in the jail.
That night I slept to the sawing of immense
machines constructing: saws in circles slicing
white crescents, shafts and blocks, as if Tyre and Sidon
were being reconstructed from salt *ab ovo*
in Boston to confound the intellect,
the treasonable defendant shouting: "Sell-out.
"They have had all they can have, and have ruined
so much they will not safely ruin me."

Child-Pastel of Adrienne Rich

Trained at four to read a score by Mozart,
perched on *Plutarch's Lives* to reach the keyboard,
paid a raisin for each note struck true—
the painter of your pastel has graced and hurt you,
your true touch too attuned by your James Mill father. . . .
Then round, bowl-bobbed, married, a mother, came
the season of your rash fling at playing bourgeois. . . .
Self-starved now, one loose lock tossed: "The splendid must fall—
Montaigne, you bastard!" You'll rob the arsenal
to feed the needy, Toussaint, Fanon, Malcolm,
the Revolution's *mutilés de guerre*,
shirtless ones dying, or killing on the rooftops—
disabled veteran, how long will you bay with the hounds
and beat time with crutches? Your groundnote is joy.

Struggle of Non-Existence

Here on the bank where Darwin found his fair one,
and thirty kinds of weeds of the wood in flower,
and a blue shirt, a blue shirt, and our love-beads
rattling together to tell us we are young—
we found the fume-gray thistle far-gone in flower. . . .
God works inside us like the plowman worm
turning a soil that must have lost much sweetness
since Eden when the funk of Abel proved
the one thing worse than war is massacre. . . .
Man turns dimwit quicker than the mayfly,
fast goes the lucid moment of love-believed;
tissue sings to sinew, "Passerby . . .
dying beside you, I feel the live blood simmer
in our hands, and know we are alive."

The Revolution

The roaddust blinds us, tactics grow occult,
the terror of spending the summer with a child,
the revolution has happened in the mind,
a fear of stopping—when the soul, even the soul
of ruin, leaves a country, the country dies. . . .
"We're in a prerevolutionary situation
at Berkeley, an incredible, refreshing relief
from your rather hot-house, good prep-school Harvard riots.
The main thing is our exposure to politics;
whether this a priori will determine
the revolutionary's murder in the streets,
or the death of the haves by the have-nots, I don't know;
but anyway you should be in on it—
only in imagination can we lose the battle."

Youth

They go into the world, innocent, wordy, called
in all the directions I would want to go,
multiplying their twenties to the year 2000.
When I was young and closer to the Faith,
half my friends were leftists and professors
who could read the news when they were born,
they knew that kings must either reign or die.
Many a youth will turn from student to tiger,
seeking his final quarry in the grave—
our blasphemous, unavoidable last Mother
nourished on slow, cold debaucheries,
the bitter, dry pelt of feline undulation—
in her harlot's door of colored beads, she holds
youth old as Michelangelo to her bosom.

Trunks

The tree trunks in our headlights are bright white worms,
inside a truck-shed, white tires are hung like paintings;
the best photographer dare not retouch them—
not everyone accepts their claim to greatness.
If blood doesn't spurt from my eyelashes, when
I meet a work of art, it isn't art—
too much persuasion is famine, enough a miracle,
yet God is good, he sees us all as straw dogs.
Even the toothless, trodden worm can writhe—
in the night-moment, even a halt-pacifist,
nursed on leaflets and wheat-germ, hears the drum-step
of his kind whistle like geese in converging lines,
the police weeping in their fog of Mace,
while he plants the black flag of anarchy and peace.

156

For Mary McCarthy 1

Your eight-inch softwood, starblue floorboard, your house
sawn for some deadport Revolutionary squire. . . .
A friendly white horse doing small-point, smiling,
the weathered yeoman loveliness of a duchess,
enlightenment in our dark age though Irish,
our Diana, rash to awkwardness. . . .
Whose will-shot arrows sing cleaner through the pelt?
Have I said *will*, and not intelligence?
Leaving you I hear your mind, mind, mind,
stinging the foundation-termites, stinging
insistently with a battering ram's brass head of brass. . . .
I hide my shyness in bluster; you align
words more fairly, eighty percent on target—
we can only meet in the bare air.

For Mary McCarthy 2

"Dear Mary, with her usual motherly
solicitude for the lost overdog. . . ."
You sometimes seemed to stand by a white horse,
a Dürer Saint Joan armed by your college and by
that rougher university, the world. . . .
Since your travels, the horse is firmly yours;
you stare off airily through our mundane gossip
and still more mundane virtue, listen puzzled,
groan to yourself, and blurt an ice-clear sentence—
one hand, for solace, toying with the horse's mane. . . .
The immortals are all about us and above us;
for us *immortal* means another book;
there are too many . . . with us, the music stops;
the first violin stops to wipe the sweat from his brow.

For Mary McCarthy 3

"*The land going down to the lake was choked with wild rose,*
the sunset orchards were scarlet, the high swans, drunk
on making love, had bathed their aching heads;
the water was rebirth at first, then a winter:
no sun, or flower, or even hue for shadow. . . .
Exhaust and airconditioning klir in the city. . . .
The real motive for my trip is dentistry,
a descending scale: long ago, I used to drive
to New York to see a lover, next the analyst,
an editor, then a lawyer . . . time's dwindling choice.
But I can't quite make students all Seven Ages of Man.
Work means working; I fear I am one of the few
sane people living . . . not too stunning a sensation—
They want something different from understanding: belief."

The Going Generation

Our going generation; there are days
of pardon . . . perhaps to go on living in
the old United States of William James,
its once reposeful, now querulous, optimism.
I hear the catbird's coloratura cluck
singing fuck, fuck above the brushwood racket.
The feeder deals catfood like cards to the yearling
salmon in their stockpond by the falls.
Grace-days . . . it is less than heaven, our shelving
bulkhead of lawn black with binoculars,
eyelashes in the lenses that magnify
the rising bosom of the moon—drink, drink, and pitch
the old rings of Saturn like horseshoes round the light-globe . .
in some tosses, it's heads you win and tails I lose.

158

Penelope

Manet's bourgeois husband takes the tiller at Cannes,
the sea is right, the virgin's cocky boater,
naive as the moon, streams with heartstring ribbons—
as if Ulysses were her husband for the Sunday. . . .
"Do clothes make the man, or a man the clothes?"
Ulysses whistles—enters his empty household,
the deserted hollowness of its polish,
cellar, womb, growths—heartless philanderer,
he wants his Penelope, and still pretends
he can change a silk purse to a sow's ear, thinks
something like this, or something not like this:
"How many a brave heart drowned on monologue
revives on ass, and lives for alcohol. . . .
Is it silk cuts scissors, or scissors silk?"

Ulysses

Shakespeare stand-ins, same string hair, gay, dirty . . .
there's a new poetry in the air, it's youth's
patent, lust coolly led on by innocence—
late-flowering Garden, far from Eden fallen,
and still fair! None chooses as his model
Ulysses landhugging from port to port for girls . . .
his marriage a cover for the underworld,
dark harbor of suctions and the second chance.
He won Nausicaa twenty years too late. . . .
Scarred husband and wife sit naked, one Greek smile,
thinking *we were bound to fall in love*
if only we stayed married long enough—
because our ships are burned and all friends lost.
How we wish we were friends with half our friends!

Before Repeal

O our repose, the goat's diminishing day—
the Romantic who sings, sings not in vain
Don Giovanni's farcical, brute leap. . . .
In New Orleans and just married, both our pajamas
hung out of reach and wrestling with the moisture
caught on the leather blade of the central fan—
our generation bred to drink the ocean
in the all-possible before Repeal;
all the girls were under twenty, and the boys
unearthly with the white blond hair of girls,
crawling the swimming pool's robin-egg sky.
Autumn deepens that color, warms vine and wire,
the ant's cool, amber, hyperthyroid eye,
grapes tanning on our tried entanglements.

Thanksgiving 1660 or 1960

When life grows shorter and daylightsaving dies—
God's couples marched in arms to harvest-home
and Plymouth's communal distilleries . . .
three days they lay at peace with God and beast. . . .
I reel from Thanksgiving midday into night:
the young are mobile, friends of the tossed waste leaf,
bellbottom, barefoot, Christendom's wild hair—
words are what get in the way of what they say.
None sleeps with the same girl twice, or marches homeward
keeping the beat of her arterial vein,
or hears the cello grumbling in her garden.
The sleeper has learned karate—Revolution,
drugging her terrible premenstrual cramps,
marches with unbra'd breasts to storm the city.

For Aunt Sarah

You never had the constitution to quarrel:
poised, warm and cool, distrusting hair and Hamlets,
yet infinitely kind—in short a lady,
still reaching for the turn of the century,
your youth in the solid golden age, when means
needed only to follow the golden mean
to love and care for the world; when businessmen
and their ancillary statesmen willingly gave up
health, wealth and pleasure for the gall of office—
converts to their only fiction, God.
But this new age? "They have no fun," you say. . . .
We've quarreled lightly almost fifty years,
Dear, long enough to know how high our pulse beats, while the
    young
wish to stand in our shoes before we've left them.

Flight in the Rain

Why did I say, I'm not afraid of flying,
death has no meaning in imagination?
Too much gets published without imagination. . . .
Tonight: the wing-tilt, air-bounce upright, lighted
Long Island mainstreets flashed like dice on the window;
raindrops, gut troutlines wriggling on the window—
the landing no landing—low circling at snailspace
exhausting a world of suburban similars. . . .
My delicate stomach says, *You were.* Says, *Pray*—
my mismanaged life incorrigible—
prayer can live without faith. God is *déjà vû,*
He hears the sparrow fall, heard years from here
in Rio, one propeller clunking off,
my *Deo gracias* on the puking runway.

Blizzard in Cambridge

Risen from the blindness of teaching to bright snow,
everything mechanical stopped dead,
taxis no-fares . . . *the wheels grow hot from driving—*
ice-eyelashes, in my spring coat; the subway
too jammed and late to stop for passengers;
snow-trekking the mile from subway end to airport . . .
to all-flights-canceled, fighting queues congealed
to telephones out of order, stamping buses,
rich, stranded New Yorkers staring with the wild, mild eyes
of steers at the foreign subway—then the train home,
jolting with stately grumbling: an hour in Providence,
in New Haven . . . the Bible. In darkness seeing
white arsenic numbers on the tail of a downed plane,
the smokestacks of abandoned fieldguns burning skyward.

The Heavenly Rain

Man at the root of everything he builds;
no nature, except the human, loves New York—
the clerk won't prove Aseity's existence
busing from helpless cause to helpless cause. . . .
The rain falls down from heaven, and heaven keeps
her noble distance, the dancer is seen not heard.
The rain falls, and the soil swims up to breathe;
a squatter sumac shafted in cement
flirts wet leaves skyward like the Firebird.
Two girls clasp hands in a clamshell courtyard, watch
the weed of the sumac failing visibly;
the girls age not, are always last year's girls
waiting for tomorrow's storm to wash
the fallen leaf, turned scarlet, back to green.

Misanthrope and Painter

"I'm *the misanthrope*, a woman who hates men—
men may be smarter but we are stronger.
We hate you mostly for the other woman,
yet even Desdemona dreams a faithless
Cassio will step into Othello's bed.
I am a painter, not a woman painter.
The only way Helen can fix her lyric palette
would be to throw herself under a truck.
Don't sell me your personality garbage, Baby;
when Rembrandt painted the last red spot on the nose
of a clown or Rembrandt, he disappeared in the paint.
That's my technique . . . I'm not nothing, Baby;
Rothko is invisible when I'm in the room.
You may have *joie de vivre*, but you're not twenty."

Redskin

Unsheathed, you unexpectedly go redskin,
except for two white torches, fruits of summer,
woman's headlights to guide us through the dark
to love the body, the only love man is.
Women look natural stripped to flesh, not man
equipped with his redemptive bat and balls—
Renoir, paralyzed, painted with his penis.
Endless, aimless consecutive sentences. . . .
Rain claws the skylight, a thousand fingernails,
icy, poorly circulating fingers
trickling all night from heaven to our skins . . .
our bodies sunburnt in the staining dawn. . . .
At wrath-break, when earth and ocean merge,
who wants to hold his weapon to the whale?

Thirst

The chilled glass of julep blows to pollen,
A cold wind, snow-touched, fans our streaming backs,
blows in and in, a thousand snow-years back,
above the Hudson's essence-steaming back,
the Great Arriviste in the metropolis. . . .
We have licked the acid of the saltmarsh,
salt craves its weight in water—thirst without bottom.
Your hand, a small monkey's, cannot lift your drink—
there'll be no more. We gasp, and fall asleep—
love's dissolution . . . we breathe no air from it,
only my heavy, secret and sad sighs.
Where is the tunnel that led to our only exit,
a hole soon filled with twenty slides of snow?
We were joined in love a thousand snow-years back.

New York

We must have got a lift once from New York
seven years back or so, it's hard to think,
gone like my Greek and box for butterflies. . . .
A pilgrim comes here from the outlands, Trinidad,
Port of Spain seeking a sister metropolis—
lands here, knowing nothing, strapped and twenty—
to parade the streets of wonder. . . . Plateglass
displays look like nightclubs blocks away;
each nightclub is heaven with a liveried tariff,
all the money, all the connection. . . . You have none,
you are triggered by the liberated girl,
whipped to that not unconquerable barricade,
by our first categorical imperative, "Move,
you bastard, do you want to live forever?"

164

Sounds in the Night

Nothing new in them yet their old tune startles;
asked to adapt, they swear they cannot swerve:
machines are our only servants bound to serve,
metal, mortal and mechanical,
a dissonance more varied than New York birds
winging their clatter through the night air dirt.
Sleepless I drink their love, if it is love.
Miles below me, luminous on the night,
some simple court of wall-brick windowless,
and the grass-conservative cry of the cat in heat—
Who cares if the running stream is sometimes stopped—
inexhaustible the springs from which I flow.
Cats will be here when man is prehistory,
gone as Prohibition or mahjong.

Dream of Leak and Terra-Cotta

I would drown if I crossed these terra-cotta tiles—
drops strike with the tock of a townhall clock,
hitting more steadily than the minute hand—
like industry's doggéd, clogged pollution.
The toilet paper is squirled like a Moslem tile,
in the basin, a sad ringlet of my pubic hair—
an overweight, crested bathmat, squeezed
to a pierced pipe, and alchemized to water,
sprinkling bright drops of gin, dime-size and silver—
everything man-made is about to change to water. . . .
When I lift the window, there was a view,
a green meadow pointing to a greener meadow,
to dogs, to deer, Diana out in war-skirt . . .
heaven paved with terra-cotta tile.

Fever

Desultory, sour commercial September
lies like a mustard plaster on the back—
Pavlov's dogs, when tortured, turned neurotics. . . .
If I see something unbelievable in the city,
it is the woman shopper out in war-paint—
the druggist smiles etherealized in glass. . . .
Sometimes, my mind is a rocked and dangerous bell;
I climb the spiral stairs to my own music,
each step more poignantly oracular,
something inhuman always rising in me—
a friend drops in the street and no one stirs.
Even if I should indiscreetly write
the perfect sentence, it isn't English—
I go to bed Lord Byron, and wake up bald.

Across the Yard: La Ignota

The soprano's bosom breathes the joy of God,
Brunhilde who could not rule her voice for God—
her stately yellow ivory window frames
haven't seen paint or putty these twenty years;
grass, dead since Kennedy, chokes the window box.
She has to sing to keep her curtains flying;
one is pink dust flipped back to scarlet lining,
the other besmirched gauze; and behind them
a blown electric heater, her footlocker with Munich
stickers stood upright for a music stand.
Her doorbell is dead. No one has to hire her.
She flings her high aria to the trash like roses. . . .
When I was lost and green, I would have given
the janitor three months' rent for this address.

Elisabeth Schwarzkopf in New York

The great still fever for Paris, Vienna, Milan;
which had more genius, grace, preoccupations?
Loss of grace is bagatelle to pay
for a niche in the Pantheon or New York—
and as for Europe, they could bring it with them.
Elisabeth Schwarzkopf sings, herself her part,
Wo ist Silvia, Die alte Marschallin,
until the historic rivers of both worlds,
the Hudson and the Danube burst their bar,
trembling like water-ivy down my spine,
from satyr's tussock to the hardened hoof. . . .
La Diva, crisped, remodelled for the boards,
roughs it with chaff and cardigan at recordings
like anyone's single and useful weekend guest.

Diamond Cutters

A terrible late October summer day;
we passed the diamond cutters and appraisers,
hole-in-the-corners on 47th Street—
trade ancient as the Ur-kings and their banks,
gambling empires for a grain of dust;
heaven in essence, crystal, hard and bright.
Herman Melville would have found a meaning,
while scuffing his final dogdays in New York,
far from cousin dogfish and white whale,
unable to slumber from his metaphysics,
his mason's chisel on the throat of stone. . . .
We were boulevarding out the hour till lunch;
our conversation was inaudible to You,
eye brighter than the uncut sun at noon.

Candlelight Lunchdate

An oldtime sweatshop, remodelled purple brick—
candlelightbulbs twinkle in stormlamp chimneys;
the *Chez Dreyfus*, Harvard. The chimneys don't smoke,
their light is cruel; we are not highschool dates.
In college we hated the middle-aged, now we,
the late middles are ten years their seniors,
caught by in their swelling stream of traffic.
Say the worst, Harvard at least speaks English,
words are given a fighting chance to speak:
your hand now unattainable was not attained.
"You used to be less noisy." I kept your discards,
hairpins, buckles and beautiful dyed hairs—
we needn't be sick in mind, or believe in God,
to love the flesh of our youth, V-mouth of the pike.

Stoodup

Light takes on a meaning in the afternoon—
diamond windows of a Madison Avenue British pub,
one is streaming noonday, the other is dull;
reds gleam in the grand glass of the sporting prints:
blue beefy faces fired by the hunt and scotch,
Old England tarted up with boor and barmaid;
these reproductions urbanize the coarse. . . .
Sometimes color lines are blurred and dim
in the great city, and exotics mate.
It is not malevolence but inertia
that prevents our meeting obligations,
your active sloth that ties my willing hands—
two windows, two reflections, one bypasser
doubled and hurrying from his double life.

168

Two Walls

(1968, MARTIN LUTHER KING'S MURDER)

Somewhere a white wall faces a white wall,
one wakes the other, the other wakes the first,
each burning with the other's borrowed splendor—
the walls, awake, are forced to go on talking,
their color looks much alike, two shadings of white,
each living in the shadow of the other.
How fine our distinctions when we cannot choose!
Don Giovanni can't stick his sword through stone,
two contracting, white stone walls—their pursuit
of happiness and his, coincident. . . .
At this point of civilisation, this point of the world,
the only satisfactory companion we
can imagine is death—this morning, skin lumping in my throat,
I lie here, heavily breathing, the soul of New York.

Abstraction

Question: why do I write? Answer: if I stop,
I might as well stop breathing—superstition
I want to write this without style or feeling—
4 a.m. to 7, I lay awake,
my mouth watering for some painless poison;
insomnia flings cowards small grains of courage,
they live to swell the overpopulation. . . .
Who has done this to me? Drink brought immortal
Faulkner, Crane and Hemingway themselves,
helped them plot on self-inspired to the end,
less awkward for their enemies than friends.
Their moment threw the dice out wrong,
or the chances befriended, not the choices—
the velocity of conversation.

Dissenting Academy

The Black Moslem's hack-moon hangs over WABC
TELEVISION, and its queue of stand-ins;
real trees, the sky-distempered, skim the heavens,
rooted in a nondescript, yellow brick tower—
my city! No zoned village curbs more coiffeured poodles,
our iron sings like a hundred kinds of birds.
The birds have left for the country. . . . In ivy-league colleges,
men breathe, and study darkens their small panes.
A professor has students to prime his pump
and wattles like a turkey to his grant—
each university is his universe. . . .
It's petty, and not worth writing home about,
why should anyone settle for New York?
Dying without death is living in a city.

Taxi Drivers

A green-leaf cushion is seat and back of my swivel-chair,
I swivel round past ceiling, walls, and locks—
an eerie study, bluegloss streaked with green.
They will never let me finish a sentence. . . .
The taxi drivers always hold the floor;
born with directions, crackling rolls of bills,
only wanting more juice to burn—unslowing
hacks condemned to keep in step with snails. . . .
How many voyagers have they talked to death—
safe from their fares in forts of gunproof plastic,
they daily run their course to the edge of culture,
the hem of Harlem. . . . I swing from wall to wall;
taxis dissect New York . . . some, unable
to see they're finished, go on into the wall.

Goiter Test, Utopia for Racoons

My goiter expert smiles like a racoon,
"O.K., you're rich and can afford to die."
He claws me a minute, claws his notes for five,
claws his notes three weeks, then claws me back;
he could crack my adam's apple like a walnut.
He washes his hands of me and licks his paws,
sipping his fountainpen for bubbly ink.
In a larger room in a greater hospital,
two racoons wear stethoscopes to count the pulse
of their geiger-counter and their thyroid scan;
they sit sipping my radioactive iodine
from a small zinc bottle with two metal straws.
What little health we have is stolen fruit.
What is the life-expectancy of a racoon?

Goiter Delirium, Werner von Usslingen

Half eggshell, half eggshell, white in a glass of water;
a whiteness swollen and doubled by the water,
soft goiters croaking in a plaster-cast,
heads flayed to the bone like Leonardo's felons,
heads thrust forward at me not to hear,
lipping with the astuteness of the deaf—
no skull so bald, this never had hair. I complain
like a bough asking severance from the dead tree—
it isn't me, I still to die and leave
my momentary thumbprint on the plaster-cast. . . .
This memento mori Dürer could have etched
or the landsknecht, Werner von Usslingen, who gave
his shield this motto, a German's faith in French:
L'ennemi de Dieu et de merci.

Under the Dentist

"When I say you *feel*, I mean you *don't*. This thing's
metaphysical not sensational:
you come here in your state of hypertension,
Bob . . . you lie quiet, be very, very good—
do you feel the jangling in your nerves?
You will feel the city jangling in your nerves,
a professor might even hear the cosmos jangle.
You watch news, the pictures will flick and jangle.
You don't have to be I.Q. or Maria Callas
to have feelings. Thinking burns out nerve;
that's why you cub professors calcify.
You got brains, why do you smoke? I stopped smoking, drinking,
not pussy . . . it's not vice. I drill here 8 to 5,
make New York at sunrise—I've got nerves."

Window-Ledge 1. The Bourgeois

Our house, forced, liberated, still on fire—
hand over hand on the noosed rope, the boy,
tanned, a cool crew haircut, nears my ledge,
smiling at me to mount his shoulders, swing
down fifty tiers of windows, two city blocks,
on that frail thread, his singed and tapering rope.
Looking down, our building is a tapered rope,
fat head, small base—Louis Philippe, his pear-face
mirrored upside-down in a silver spoon.
I must go down the rope to save my life—
I am too big in the head. I solved this in my dream:
if forced to walk to safety on a tightrope,
if my life hung on my will and skill . . . better die.
The crowd in the street is cheering, when I refuse.

172

Window-Ledge 2. Gramsci in Prison

The only light I saw was sun reflected
off other windows from 3 p.m. to 4—
like Gramsci in a Roman prison reflecting
pessimism of intelligence, optimism of will. . . .
What I dreamed is not designed to happen—
to waken on the window's sloping ledge,
it soon apparent that I will not cling
hugging my shins and whistling daylight home
through the chalk and catlight of the ancient city,
Caesar's Rome of assassins and sunsick palms—
windows reflecting lightning without heat. . . .
I lived to the vibration of fulfilment,
falling past galleried windows to my bash—
I saw the world is the same as it has been.

Five Hour Political Rally

A design of insects on the rug's red acre,
one to each ten feet like the rich in graves;
the belly is like a big watermelon seed,
each head an empty pretzel, less head than mouth,
the wings are emblems, black as the ironwork
for a Goya balcony, lure and bar to love—
the Spanish darkeyed and protected Spanish girls
exhibited by the custom that imprisons.
Insects and statesmen grapple on the carpet;
all excel, as if each were the candidate;
twenty first ballerinas are in the act.
Like insects they almost live on breath alone:
If you swallow me, I'll swallow you.

For Robert Kennedy 1925–68

Here in my workroom, in its listlessness
of Vacancy, like the old townhouse one shut for summer,
airtight and sheeted from the sun and smog,
far from the hornet yatter of his gang—
is loneliness, a thin smoke thread of vital
air. But what will anyone teach you now?
Doom was woven in your nerves, your shirt,
woven in the great clan; they too were loyal,
and you too were loyal to them, to death.
For them like a prince, you daily left your tower
to walk through dirt in your best cloth. Untouched,
alone in my Plutarchan bubble, I miss
you, you out of Plutarch, made by hand—
forever approaching our maturity.

For Robert Kennedy 2

How they hated to leave the unpremeditated
gesture of their life—the Irish in black, three rows
ranked for the future photograph, the Holy Name,
fiercely believed in then, then later held to
perhaps more fiercely in their unbelief. . . .
We were refreshed when you wisecracked through the guests,
usually somewhat woodenly, hoarsely dry. . . .
Who would believe the nesting, sexing tree swallow
would dive for eye and brain—this handbreadth insect,
navy butterfly, the harbinger of rain,
changed to a danger in the twilight? Will we
swat out the birds as ruthlessly as flies? . . .
God hunts us. Who has seen him, who will judge this killer,
his guiltless liver, kidneys, fingertips and phallus?

174

Assassin!   (*Les Enfants du Paradis*)

The swinging of a bush, a bird, a fly,
even the shadow of these grows animate,
if anyone really wants to kill anyone. . . .
He waits. I wait. *I am a writer not a leader.*
But even a paranoid can have enemies. . . .
A hero might break his spine to better purpose,
like the two *apaches* in *Enfants du Paradis*
who ambush the Baron bathing in his bath-house.
No sport. The Baron (naked) sucks his hookah.
The first killer walks offscreen to his dark game;
the second waits. It's the fear which isn't screened.
The last shot is a dead arm dangling from the tub,
the assassin snaps and pockets the bowl of the hookah . . .
to prove in recollection that something gave.

For Eugene McCarthy
    (JULY, 1968)
I love you so. . . . Gone? Who will swear you wouldn't
have done good to the country, that fulfilment wouldn't
have done good to you—the father, as Freud says:
you? We've so little faith that anyone
ever makes anything better . . . the same and less—
ambition only makes the ambitious great.
The state lifts us, we cannot raise the state. . . . All
was yours though, lining down the balls for hours,
freedom of the hollow bowling-alley,
the thundered strikes, the boys. . . . Picking a quarrel
with you is like picking the petals of the daisy—
the game, the passing crowds, the rapid young
still brand your hand with sunflecks . . . coldly willing
to smash the ball past those who bought the park.

Ocean

Mostly its color must adulterate,
sway, swelter; earth stands firm and not the sea,
one substance everywhere divisible,
great bosom of salt. It floats us—less and less
usable now we can fly like the angels.
We cannot stay alive without the ocean;
I think all marriages are like the ocean:
one part oxygen mates two parts hydrogen,
as if the formula existed everywhere
in us, as in the numinous Parnassus of chemistry.
The statesman mutters, "The problems of politics
are nothing. . . ." He was thinking of his marriage—
uncontrollable, law-ravaged like the ocean . . . God is
H_2O Who must forgive us for having lived.

Dream, the Republican Convention

That night the mustard bush and goldenrod
and more unlikely yellows trod a spiral,
clasped in eviscerating blue china vases
like friendly snakes embracing—cool not cold. . . .
Brotherly, stacked and mean, the great Convention
throws out Americana like dead flowers:
choices, at best, that hurt and cannot cure;
many are chosen, and too few were called. . . .
And yet again, I see the yellow bush rise,
the golds of the goldenrod eclipse their vase
(each summer the young breasts escape the ribcage)
a formation, I suppose, beyond the easel.
What can be is only what will be—
the sun warms the mortician, unpolluted.

176

Flaw

My old eye-flaw sprouting bits and strings
gliding like dragon-kites in the Midwestern sky—
I am afraid to look closely, and count them;
today I am exhausted and afraid.
I look through the window at unbroken white cloud,
and see in it my many flaws are one,
a flaw with a tail the color of shed skin,
inaudible rattle of the rattler's disks.
God is design, even our ugliness
is the goodness of his will. It gives me warning,
the first scrape of the Thunderer's fingernail. . . .
Faust's soul-sale was perhaps to leave the earth,
yet death is sweeter, weariness almost lets
me taste its sweetness none will ever taste.

After the Democratic Convention

Life, hope, they conquer death, generally, always;
and if the steamroller goes over the flower, the flower dies.
Some are more solid earth; they stood in lines,
blouse and helmet, a creamy de luxe sky-blue—
their music savage and ephemeral.
After five nights of Chicago: police and mob,
I am so tired and had, clichés are wisdom,
the clichés of paranoia. . . . Home in Maine,
the fall of the high tide waves is a straggling, joshing
mell of police . . . they're on the march for me. . . .
How slender and graceful, the double line of trees,
slender, graceful, irregular and underweight,
the young in black folk-fire circles below the trees—
under their shadow, the green grass turns to hay.

From Prague 1968

Once between 6 and 7 a.m. at Harvard, we counted
ten jets, or maybe forty, one thunder-rivet
no one could sleep through, though many will.
In Prague on the eve of the *Liberation*, you woke
to the Russian troop-planes landing, chain on anvil,
and thought you were back at Harvard. I wish you were,
up and out on our tramp through the one museum.
You thought the best paintings between the Sienese
and Haitians were photographs. We've kept
up flirting since the fall of Harry Truman.
Even an old fool is flattered by an old girl,
tights, shoes, shirts, pinkthings, blackthings, my watch, your bra,
untidy exposures that cannot clash. . . . We lay,
talking without any need to say.

Election Night

Election Night, last night's Election Night,
without drinks, television or my friend—
today I wore my blue knitted tie to class.
No one understood that blue meant black. . . .
My daughter telephones me from New York,
she talks *New Statesman*, "Then you are a cop-out. Isn't
not voting Humphrey a vote for Nixon and Wallace?"
And I, "Not voting Nixon is my vote for Humphrey."
It's funny-awkward; I don't come off too well;
"You mustn't tease me, they clubbed McCarthy's pressroom."
We must rouse our broken forces and save the country:
I even said this in public. The beaten player
opens his wounds and hungers for the blood-feud
hidden like contraband and loved like whisky.

178

After the Election: From Frank Parker's Loft

We remember watching old Marshal Joffre or Foche
chauffeured in Roman triumph, though French, through Boston—
the same small, pawky streets, the Back Bay station,
though most of Boston's now a builders' dream,
white, unspoiled and blank. Here nothing has slid
since 1925. The Prudential Building
that saved so many incomes, here saves nothing.
From your window we see the *Thread and Needle Shoppe*,
where we stole a bad fifteen-dollar microscope,
and failed to make them pay back fifteen dollars. . . .
On the starry thruways headlights twinkle
from Portland, Maine to Portland, Oregon.
Nobody has won, nobody has lost;
will the election-winners ever pay us back?

Puzzle

A broad doorway, garage or warehouse door,
an asthmatic man panting into it to hide—
helpless place to hide, though two or three
off-duty policemen in earphones banquet on stools. . . .
The old team have the city. In an open car
elected and loser stand reflecting our smiles—
no insurance policy will accept them.
Disappointed we discover they're twins.
A voice moves like the ribs of a rake to reform the city.
Enamelled with joy and speechless with affliction—
Fra Angelico's *Last Judgment* . . . two
of the elect, two angels more restless than the rest,
swoop along a battlemented street
blank with the cobbled ennui of feudal Florence.

West Side Sabbath

(BREAKFAST)

WIFE, in her tower of *The New York Times*;
HUSBAND, rewriting his engagement-book. . . .
WIFE: Nixon's in trouble. HUSBAND: Another family
brawl? WIFE: Nixon has profounder troubles.
HUSBAND: You mean our National Peace Offensive?
WIFE: *Entre autres.* HUSBAND: When Nixon weighs in,
does he outweigh *The New York Sunday Times*?
WIFE: Say that twice, and I'll fly to San Juan with Bruce. . . .
Is our chance a monochrome Socialism,
Robespierre's gunpoint equality,
privilege slashed to a margin of survival?
Or the Student-Left's casually defined
anarchists' faith in playing the full deck—
who wants the monks without the fucking Maypole?

Eating Out Alone

The loneliness inside me is a place,
Harvard where no one might always be someone.
When we're alone people we run from change
to the mysterious and beautiful—
I am eating alone at a small white table,
visible, ignored . . . the moment that tries the soul,
an explorer going blind in polar whiteness.
Yet everyone who is seated is a lay,
or Paul Claudel, at the next table declaiming:
"*L'Académie Groton, eh, c'est une école des cochons.*"
He soars from murdered English to killing French,
no word unheard, no sentence understood—
a vocabulary to mortify Racine . . .
the minotaur steaming in a maze of eloquence.

Painter

"I said you are only keeping me here
in the hospital, lying to my parents
and saying I am madder than I am,
because you only want to keep me here,
squeezing my last dollar to the pennies—
I'm saner than anyone in the hospital.
I had to say what every madman says—
a black phrase, *the sleep of reason mothers monsters*. . . .
When I am painting the canvas is a person;
all I do, each blot and line's alive,
when I am finished, it is shit on the canvas. . . .
But in his sketches more finished than his oils,
sketches made *after* he did those masterpieces,
Constable can make us *see* the breeze . . ."

In the American Grain

"Ninth grade, and bicycling the Jersey highways:
I am a writer. I was half-wasp already,
I changed my shirt and trousers twice a day.
My poems came back . . . often rejected, though never
forgotten in New York, this Jewish state
with insomniac minorities.
I am sick of the enlightenment:
what Wall Street prints, the mafia distributes;
when talent starves in a garret, they buy the garret.
Bill Williams made less than Bandaids on his writing,
he could never write the King's English of *The New Yorker*.
I am not William Carlos Williams. He
knew the germ on every flower, and saw
the snake is a petty, rather pathetic creature."

Publication Day

"Dear Robert: I wish you were not a complete stranger,
I wish I knew something more about your mercy,
could total your minimum capacity
for empathy—this varies so much from genius.
Can you fellow-suffer for a turned-down book?
Can you see through your tragic vision, and
have patience with one isolated heart?
Do you only suffer for other famous people,
and socially comforting non-entities?
Has the thistle of failure a place in your affection?
It's important to know these things; in your equestrian
portrait by Mailer, I don't find these things. . . .
I write as a woman flung from a sinking ship—
one raft in the distance . . . you represent that raft."

Loser

"Now I'm almost impotent, I'm almost faithful;
that's why I stay here boozing off my marriage,
it has lasted more than thirty years'
nightly immersion in the acid bath.
The girl in bed was a mouth with two elastics,
a slit of blue daylight below the blowing shade—
my wife sat reading Simone de Beauvoir till day.
All marriages are alike . . . *sagesse de crise!*
Why was her toothpaste always in my tumbler?
For a true loser any good break is verbal,
we monopolize the low cards that lose tricks—
I have my place . . . if one is put in his place
enough times, he becomes his place . . .
the flatterer's all-forgiving, wounded smile."

The Winner

I had the talent before I played the game;
I made the black moves, then the white moves,
I just muled through whole matches with myself—
it wasn't too social only mating myself. . . .
But this guy in West Berlin whispers a move in my ear,
or there's a guy with his head right over my board—
they weren't too communicative with high chess.
Are most of your friends from the chess world?
I have a few peripheral friends here and there
who are non-chess players, but it's strange,
if you start partying around, it doesn't go.
I try to broaden myself, I read the racetrack,
but it's a problem if you lose touch with life . . .
because they want two world leaders to fight it out hand to hand.

Keepsakes

"If once a winter with absent heart, you look,
then push my ingots underneath your checkstubs;
robbing children of trash was your great joke—
these are not rape, but things for Lost and Found:
bronze bosses, Arab dagger, thin true gold chain,
an ABC design almost too childish
for a child to spell. Can you still spell my name?
I was your gold mine rich with senseless power,
sluiced by your turbulent, pretentious meekness,
my passive willingness for the sullen delight.
Has too much skating cracked the ice? Do you still
swell your stomach with oracle, and say,
'Girls make things happen'—then rush to Boston with money
for first-hand exercise in this religion?"

The Just-Forties

Somewhere on the West Side with its too many
cleared lots ill-occupied with rusting cars,
I meet this innumerable acquaintance
masked in faces, though forward and familiar,
equipped for encounter like cops or Caesar's legions;
all seem to enjoy at least six men at once,
amateurs building up clienteles of love,
always one on the doorbell, another fleeing—
the Just-Forties, girls (Why is no man just forty?)
born too late for enriching memories:
President Harding, Prohibition, the boom market—
too experienced to be surprised,
and too young to know satiety,
the difficulty of giving up everything.

Under the Moon

In this wavy moonlight, we, like others,
too thoughtful clods, may learn from those we walk on:
star-nosed moles, their catatonic tunnels
and earthworks . . . only in touch with what they touch;
blind from their secret panic to dodge the limelight—
even a subway haunter could not envy
these vegetating and protective creatures,
forever falling short of man's short life. . . .
Through my fieldglasses, I aggrandize
a half-fledged robin with a speckled breast,
big as a pheasant . . . the invincible
syllogism advances from talon to talon.
No earthly ripple disturbs the moon, the ballbearing
utility of this bald and nearest planet. . . .

Moon-Landings

The moon on television never errs,
and shares the worker's fear of immigration,
a strange white goddess imprisoned in her ash,
entombed Etruscan, smiling though immortal.
We've clocked the moon; it goes from month to month
bleeding us dry, buying less and less—
chassis orbiting about the earth,
grin of heatwave, spasm of stainless steel,
gadabout with heart of chalk, unnamable
void and cold thing in the universe,
lunatic's pill with poisonous side-effects,
body whose essence is its excess baggage,
compressed like a Chinese dried caterpillar . . .
our hallucinator, the disenchantress.

Utopia

"Is Mao's China nearer the Utopia?"
"Only twelve or fifteen dynasties;
Mao still thinks it dishonorable to carry
firearms except for students, wars and birds."
"Are we altogether certain of that much here?"
"Mao is Establishment crowned to go down fanged,
old king-ape of the ape-horde preferring deference to justice."
"I prefer lying with a Canadian girl
on the American border, the belt of the earth,
each girl pretty as her Queen but not so rich."
"None must desert his cell for wife or friend."
"A wife is such a good thing I'd cry welcome,
welcome, even if she comes from hell. . . ."
"There's a strong shadow where there's too much light."

River God

The Aztecs gave their human sacrifice
credit-cards, dames, the usual pork of kings;
after a year, the king was cooled with palm-slash;
he never remembered he lost his heart—
man and the sun were succored by his blood. . . .
Mao had to find ways to economize on lepers;
each family had its leper, fed it like a pig—
if we purify, the waterlilies die?
Mao announced the people's plan for leprosy,
the lepers came bounding from the filth of hiding,
more than Ganges, or the popular cures of Christ. . . .
On dope like kings for the colorful boatride, the lepers
were launched out on the Yangtze with a thousand flowers—
the river god caught them in his arms when they drowned.

Killer Whale Tank

Even their immensity feels the hand of man. . . .
Forming himself in an S-curve before her,
swimming side by side and belly to belly
inches distant, each one stroking the other,
feather touch of a flipper across her belly;
he teases, nuzzles and lightly bites her nose,
and with a fluke titillates the vulva—
he awakes a woman. . . . With her closed mouth she rubs
his genital slit afire, and scoots away
a fraction of a second before explosion;
then, runs straight to him and will not turn aside,
seeking the common sleep that hands them back to life.
Whales meet in love and part in friendship—swoosh. . . .
The Killer's sorrow is he has no hands.

Sheik Without Six Wives in London

His whirlwind, a delirium of Eros—
English fairplay decrees *one legal wife*;
the Sheik hears the singular marriage laws
and screams . . . Henry the Eighth espoused monogamy
and shaved six wives to one. The Sheik writes postcards:
Westminster Abbey, Lambeth, House of Lords.
He writes, "Dear Lilith, English barbarity,
love Sheckle." He writes, "Dear Goneril, Dear Regan,
barbarity!" He writes, "My dear Hetaerae,
my six Rolls Royces snowed with parking tickets,
my harem zero." He sings to his last girl
knowing she wants a man, a lover and a poet,
not knowing they are mutually abhorrent—
"I am an iceberg melting in the ocean."

After the Play

"I've been married umpteen years," Ben said,
"I've walked where angels fear to tread,"
then lost his pace by popping up each second,
and held the restaurant spellbound stumbling
from the men's room seven times in twenty minutes,
to wreck his dinner, two computered dates,
and a fellow power man, fairweather friends,
gone waspish, buzzing, "This is impossible."
This, this. They left Ben confessing to the toilet. . . .
To hell with artists painting Cromwell's warts,
London bluedays, sidewalks smeared with dogmess,
pekinese and poodle, poodle and pekinese—
sometimes the palisades of garbage bags
are beautiful sunlit playgrounds of plastic balloons.

Loud conversation is sometimes overheard:
"Take Galbraith's *Affluent Society*,
we know it's cheap whiskey, he's the type
that overstructures the picnic to use his car.
It's bells for trotting teatrays on the lawn;
we've lost the freedom of the plutocrat,
once gone, he's really gone, he's bred not made."
in the pride of possession, the *New Statesman*
and the conservative have one heart.
Dark time and darker hour for a weak faith
in the Socialist, egalitarian state.
In our time of overpopulation,
the homosexual is a savior—
Karl Marx orphaned his illegitimate child.

Loser

"Father directed choir. When it paused on a Sunday,
he liked to loiter out morning with the girls;
then back to our cottage, dinner cold on the table,
Mother locked in bed devouring tabloid.
You should see him, white fringe about his ears,
bald head more biased than a billiard ball—
he never left a party. Mother left by herself—
I threw myself from her car and broke my leg. . . .
Years later, he said, 'How jolly of you to have jumped.'
He forgot me, mother replaced his name, I miss him.
When I am unhappy, I try to squeeze the hour
an hour or half-hour smaller than it is;
orphaned, I wake at midnight and pray for day—
the lovely ladies get me through the day."

Monkeys

"You can buy cooler, more humdrum pets—
a monkey deprived of his mother in the cradle
feels the want of her affection so keenly
he either pines away or masters you
by literally hanging on your neck—
no ounce of your patience or courage is misplaced;
the worst is his air of boredom and neglect,
manifested in tail-chewing and fur-plucking.
The whole species is vulnerable to killing colds,
likes straw, hay or bits of a torn blanket,
a floortray thinly covered with sawdust,
they need trapezes, shelves, old rubber tires—
any string or beam will do to set them swinging—
these charming youngsters tend to sour with age."

Churchill 1970 Retrospective

For a time the splendid person's gone
from London—farewell Franklin, Josef, Winston,
boss's cigar and worker's overalls,
his stock still falling through the Christmas boom.
No Cromwell, though death to staff when high on brandy,
he jumped their flags like checkers on the war-map—
if he stumbled as a statesman, at least he could write.
Some British officer in Libya said,
"Out here we almost prefer Rommel to Churchill;
why is the PM such a shit to Wavell?"
They painted cardboard boxes to look like planes;
Churchill painted in mufti like Van Gogh—
icon still lighted by the fires of Dresden,
a worm like other writers, though a glow-worm.

De Gaulle's Chienlit

Seldom fine words without a virtue. He
who dumbly guns his government on virtue
is like the northern star, which keeps its place,
which keeps its place, and all the stars turn to it;
asks faithfulness and sincerity, though these
may undermine authority more than treason.
He, unseeing, says: a true man acts,
then speaks, speaks in obedience to his act:
what is good for the bee is good for the swarm.
Statecraft without labor is time lost—
and gambling with statecraft? It is perilous—
as if law could be the fulfilment of love,
as if freedom might be visible—free
to piss in any direction on your lawn.

De Gaulle est Mort

"When the French public heard de Gaulle was dead,
they popped champagne on all the squares—
even for Latins it was somehow obscene.
Was he their great man? Three days later
they read in the American press he was . . .
I kept asking those student questions you hate;
I remember a Paris taxi-driver told me:
'I would have popped champagne myself. . . . At last
France has someone better than Churchill to bury;
now he's dead, we know he defied America—
or would we have ditched them anyway?'
His choirgirls were pure white angels at Notre Dame;
I felt the Egyptians really wanted to eat
Nasser—de Gaulle, much bigger, was digested."

190

Lévi-Strauss in London

Lévi-Straus, seeing two green plants in a cleft
of a cliff choosing diverse ammonites,
imagined a crevasse of millennia spanned—
when he told me this in English, our hostess spoke French;
I left the party with a severed head.
Since France gave the English their tongue, most civilized
Englishmen can muck along in French. . . .
I was so tired of camp and decoration,
so dog-tired of wanting social hope—
is *structuralism* the bridge from Marx to death?
Cézanne left his spine sticking in the landscape,
his slow brush sucked the resin from the pines;
Picasso's bullfighter's wrist for foil and flare—
they cannot fill the crack in everything God made.

Hedgehog

"All time and culture and my sorrows vocal—
I have ripened on remorse like Stilton cheese,
I regret the brush-off brilliance of my youth . . .
once conversant with French and Jean-Paul Sartre,
now too pompous to get through the doors I crashed,
lust the sublimation of my writing;
but I have never been a society-puppet,
Lady Chelsea her face lifted at eighty,
improved for profiles, paralysed for friends,
or Jacometti's disciples, who let their teeth
fall out in homage to their toothless master.
I wasn't just a fashion-dog
defiling closed doors and asking, 'Am I in?'
No fool can pick me up and comb my quills."

Verlaine, Etc.

The tender Falstaffian ugh of Verlaine,
I who have no mind have more than you. . . . .
Are only drunken words cold sober true?
Paul Valéry's assault on modesty,
To be understood is the worst disaster.
Aside from money, literary success
was small compensation for their vanity:
to be condemned by people who never read them,
to have been useful to poets devoid of talent.
Do we like Auden want a hundred mute admirers,
or the daily surf of spit and fanmail from all
the known shores tiding in and out? . . .
The muse is a loser, she is sort of sad dirty—
publication might just scour her clean.

Onionskin

It's fancy functional things love us best;
not butterfly useless or austere with use,
they touched my body to assume a body—
my half-pound silver ticker with two bopped lids,
whose splinter lever nicked my thumbnail, and set
time moving from six a.m. to six p.m.—
twice daily time stopped and its thin hands.
It goes a-begging, without me, it is lost.
Where is grandfather's gold snakehead watchchain?
The onionskin typing paper I bought by mistake
in Bucksport Maine last August? The last sheet
creasing cuts my finger and seems to scream
as if *Fortuna* bled in the white wood
and felt the bloody gash that brought me life.

The Nihilist as Hero

"All our French poets can turn an inspired line;
who has written six passable in sequence?"
said Valéry. That was a happy day for Satan. . . .
I want words meat-hooked from the living steer,
but a cold flame of tinfoil licks the metal log,
beautiful unchanging fire of childhood
betraying a monotony of vision. . . .
Life by definition breeds on change,
each season we scrap new cars and wars and women.
But sometimes when I am ill or delicate,
the pinched flame of my match turns unchanging green,
a cornstalk in green tails and seeded tassel. . . .
A nihilist has to live in the world as is,
gazing the impassable summit to rubble.

In the Back Stacks

(PUBLICATION DAY)

My lines swell up and spank like the bow of a yacht. . . .
Outside, no break-through for the Broadway bookstores,
outside, the higher voltage of studenten,
the Revolution seeking her professor. . . .
It's life in death to be typed, bound and delivered,
lie on reserve like the Harvard *British Poets*,
hanged for keeping meter. They died with Keats.
Is it enough to be a piece of thread
in the line from King David to Hart Crane?
We talked such junk all summer behind the stacks,
while the books lay incommunicado.
The anthology holds up without us,
outlasts the brass of Cleopatra's cheeks—
everything printed will come to these back stacks.

Reading Myself

Like thousands, I took just pride and more than just,
struck matches that brought my blood to a boil;
I memorized the tricks to set the river on fire—
somehow never wrote something to go back to.
Can I suppose I am finished with wax flowers
and have earned my grass on the minor slopes of Parnassus. . . .
No honeycomb is built without a bee
adding circle to circle, cell to cell,
the wax and honey of a mausoleum—
this round dome proves its maker is alive;
the corpse of the insect lives embalmed in honey,
prays that its perishable work live long
enough for the sweet-tooth bear to desecrate—
this open book . . . my open coffin.

Last Things, Black Pines at 4 a.m.

Imperfect enough once for all at thirty,
in his last days Van Gogh painted as if
he were hurling everything he had: clothes,
bed and furniture against the door
to keep out a robber—he would have roughened
my black pines imperceptibly withdrawing
from the blue back cold of morning sky,
black pines disengaging from blue ice—
for imperfection is the language of art.
Even the best writer in his best lines
is incurably imperfect, crying for truth, knowledge,
honesty, inspiration he cannot have—
after a show of effort, Valéry
and Trollope the huntsman are happy to drop out.

Playing Ball with the Critic

(FOR RICHARD BLACKMUR)

Writers can be taught to return the ball
to the police, smile and even like it;
the critics like it, smile, kick back the ball.
Our hurt blue muscles work like testicles;
Low will we learn to duck and block the knock?
Is it a form of a force, or sentiment for form?
Your vision lacerates your syntax.
The logic is zealotry . . . In your first, best, book,
you don't distance yourself from the oddities of life. . . .
I wish I could saunter the grassy streets of old New York,
becoming every object I looked at,
stop for the unhurried, hear old Walt Whitman:
"If you will lend me a dollar, you will help
immortality to stumble on."

Outlaws, a Goodbye to Sidney Nolan

I see the pale, late glaze of an afternoon,
and chopped French conscripts of World War II
in stumps and berets playing *boules* at Pau—
what's more innocent than honorable foemen
giving their lives to kill the innocent?
Your Ned Kelly mugged and bloodied at Barracks Hall . . .
"My blood spoils the lustre of the paint on their gatepost;
when the outlaw reigns, your pockets swell;
it's double pay and double country girls. . . ."
Two rootstumps sit upright like skeletons of geese
sailing the outtide Penobscot on a saddle of drift;
five cormorants, their wing-noise like panting hounds—
Old Hand, we sometimes feel a frenzy to talk,
but truth, alas, is the father of knowing something.

Grasshoppers, for Stanley Kunitz 1970

Who else grew up in the shadow of your Worcester, Mass?
Why do I wake with a start of pathos to fear,
half-lifeless and groaning my andante—
see my no-Jew boarding school near Worcester,
class of '35 whittling . . . *our 35th*;
our pre-Prohibition summer cottage,
Buzzards Bay killing the grass for our croquet,
my homemade cases for fled skunk and turtle,
the old world black tie dinner without wine,
the lost generation sunset, its big red rose?
It is our healthy fifty years we've lost,
one's chance to break in print and love his daughter. . . .
We say the blades of grass are hay, and sing
the Joyful the creatures find no word to sing.

For Elizabeth Bishop (twenty-five years) 1. Water

At Stonington each morning boatloads of hands
cruise off for the granite quarry on the island,
leaving dozens of bleak white frame houses stuck
like oyster shells on the hill of rock. Remember?
We sit on the slab of rock. From this distance in time,
it seems the color of iris, rotting and turning purpler,
but it is only the usual gray rock
turning fresh green when drenched by the sea. . . .
The sea flaked the rock at our feet, kept lapping the matchstick
mazes of weirs where fish for bait were trapped.
You dreamed you were a mermaid clinging to a wharfpile,
trying to pull the barnacles with your hands.
We wish our two souls might return like gulls to the rock.
In the end, the water was too cold for us.

For Elizabeth Bishop 2. Castine Maine

Teenage patched jeans and softball—the Castine Common
looks like a cover for *The American Boy.*
My twelve-foot cedar hedge screens out the human.
North & South, Yarmouth to Rio, one Atlantic—
you've never found another place to live,
bound by your giant memory to one known longitude.
Britain's Georges rule your horoscope;
long live mad George Three in cap and bells,
king in your Nova Scotia, nowhere else—
a whitebeard, deaf and blind, singing Church of England
hymns he accompanied on his harpsichord.
"I wish I were a horse," you say, "or a Sicilian
sitting in my own Greenwich Village bar,
standing drinks . . . and never going outdoors."

For Elizabeth Bishop 3. Letter with Poems for Letter with Poems

"You are right to worry, only please DON'T,
though I'm pretty worried myself. I've somehow got
into the worst situation I've ever
had to cope with. I can't see the way out.
Cal, have you ever gone through caves?
I did in Mexico, and hated them.
I haven't done the famous one near here. . . .
Finally after hours of stumbling along,
you see daylight ahead, a faint blue glimmer;
air never looked so beautiful before.
That is what I feel I'm waiting for:
a faintest glimmer I am going to get out
somehow alive from this. Your last letter helped,
like being mailed a lantern or a spiked stick."

For Elizabeth Bishop 4

The new painting must live on iron rations,
rushed brushstrokes, indestructible paint-mix,
fluorescent lofts instead of French *plein air*.
Albert Ryder let his crackled amber moonscapes
ripen in sunlight. His painting was repainting,
his tiniest work weighs heavy in the hand.
Who is killed if the horseman never cry halt?
Have you seen an inchworm crawl on a leaf,
cling to the very end, revolve in air,
feeling for something to reach to something? Do
you still hang your words in air, ten years
unfinished, glued to your notice board, with gaps
or empties for the unimaginable phrase—
unerring Muse who makes the casual perfect?

Remembrance Day, London 1970's

Flipping the *Sundays* for notice of my new book,
I lost my place to a tall girl, a spine and ribs;
she bought every paper, even *News of the World*—
she had reason, her face on every front page:
Olympic runner, Lillian Board, and twenty,
told yesterday she is a cancer victim. . . .
In my coat I found a leaflet: "Our beloved
Ruth Fox . . . her first and last book, *Catch or Key,*
Journeys to far off lands or strolls at home,
was read by Frances Mintern Jones at the service
last Friday in the New England Poetry Club. . . ."
The remembered live, bagpipers in tan kilts,
their old officers in black suit, bowler and poppy,
their daughters on the sidewalk keeping their step.

Women, Children, Babies, Cows, Cats

"It was at My Lai or Sonmy or something,
it was this afternoon. . . . We had these orders,
we had all night to think about it—
we was to burn and kill, then there'd be nothing
standing, women, children, babies, cows, cats. . . .
As soon as we hopped the choppers, we started shooting.
I remember . . . as we was coming up upon one area
in Pinkville, a man with a gun . . . running—this lady . . .
Lieutenant LaGuerre said, 'Shoot her.' I said,
'You shoot her, I don't want to shoot no lady.'
She had one foot in the door. . . . When I turned her,
there was this little one-month-year-old baby
I thought was her gun. It kind of cracked me up."

Identification in Belfast

(I.R.A. BOMBING)

The British Army now carries two rifles,
one with rubber rabbit-pellets for children,
the other's of course for the Provisionals. . . .
"When they first showed me the boy, I thought oh good,
it's not him because he is a blonde—
I imagine his hair was singed dark by the bomb.
He had nothing on him to identify him,
except this box of joke trick matches;
he liked to have then on him, even at mass.
The police were unhurried and wonderful,
they let me go on trying to strike a match . . .
I just wouldn't stop—you cling to anything—
I couldn't believe I couldn't light one match—
only joke-matches. . . . Then I knew he was Richard."

Non-Violent

In the sick days of the code duello,
any quick killer could have called you out—
a million Spanish war dead, ninetenths murdered—
Viva la guerra civil, viva la muerte!
As boys we never fell in the hole to China—
few of us fell in wars, our unnegotiable
flag still floating the seven seas like a bond. . . .
Better fight to keep love, or milk bottles made of glass,
than go pluming as crusaders from left to right . . .
in the war of words, the lung of infinitude.
I must either be Christian or non-violent;
past history is immobile in our committed hands,
till Death drops his white marble scythe—Brother,
one skeleton among our skeletons.

Sound Mind, Sound Body

Mens sana? O at last; from twenty years
annual mania, their chronic adolescence—
mens sana in corpore insano.
Will I reach three score ten, or drop
the work half through? Each new birthday is the last?
Death is final and though fly-by-night,
the dirty crown on a sound fingernail.
On healthy days, I fall asleep mid-chapter—
death made Attila die of a nosebleed
on the first night of his child-bride. I linger,
I sun without sweating, hear out the old,
live on the dirt of family chronicle.
The married swallows on my work-barn scent
my kindred weakness, dare swoop me from their nest.

Those Older *1*

They won't stay gone, and stare with triumphant torpor,
as if held in my fieldglasses' fog and enlargement,
in garments washed by the rainbow, and formal with time,
elders once loved by older elders in a Maytime
invisible to us as the Hittites. I'm too old
to date their coming or going—those *late* people:
Old Aunt Sarah and Cousin Belle. God stamped
them with one maiden name *for life*—blood-rich,
and constellations from the dancing heart.
Our first to die . . . so odd and light and dry . . .
children from a child's lost world . . . they left
hooded in snail-shells, the unassailable
deafness of their formidable asperity—
our girls . . . less than a toy, and more than a flower.

Those Older *2*

No fence stands up between death and his object,
the guillotine sings the hollow green wilderness—
those older . . . I have had them fifty years;
they are gone astraying down a backward street,
not hearing the Dutchblight fritter the green elm—
old prunes and tarbone trees vulnerable to a breath,
forgetting why they put down roots near us to chill
a generation who feared exercise.
And I face faceless lines of white frame houses,
sanded, stranded, undarkened by shade or shutter . . .
mass military graveyard of those before us,
rich and poor, no trees in the sky—one white
stone multiplied a thousandfold and too close—
if I pass quickly, they melt to a field of snow.

I. A. Richards 1. Goodbye Earth

Sky-high on the cover of *Goodbye Earth*,
you flash and zigzag like a large hummingbird—
heavy socks and climber's knickerbockers,
sleeves rolled, shirt open at the throat;
an upended pick, your prisoner's ball and chain,
penetentially attached to your wrist.
Here while you take your breath, enthused, I see
the imperishable Byronics of the Swiss Alps
change to the landscape for your portrait, like you
casual, unconventional, innocent . . . earned
by gratuitous rashness and serpentine hesitation.
It is not a picture but a problem—
you know you will move on; the absolute,
bald peaks, glare-ice, malignly beckons . . . goodbye earth.

I. A. Richards 2. Death

This, our one intimate metaphysical—
today, tomorrow, death looks fairly on all.
Ivor, you knew the matter with this subject,
"My vanity won't let me believe in my death.
In our generous world-throw, ought but vanity,
death never catches those life speeds." You thought,
"A doubtful suicide should choose the ocean;
who knows, he might reach the other side?
If my coin falls heads, I'll see the other side. . . .
We still go foothill shuffling every weekend;
but climbing's dull past sixty unless you risk you life."
Hob-Alpine Spirit, you saved so much illusion
by changing its false coin to words—your shadow
on the blind bright heights . . . absconds to air.

For John Berryman 1

I feel I know what you have worked through, you
know what I have worked through—we are words;
John, we used the language as if we made it.
Luck threw up the coin, and the plot swallowed,
monster yawning for its mess of potage.
Ah privacy, as if we had preferred mounting
some rock by a mossy stream and counting the sheep . . .
to fame that renews the soul but not the heart.
The out-tide flings up wonders: rivers, linguini,
beercans, mussels, bloodstreams; how gaily they gallop
to catch the ebb—Herbert, Thoreau, Pascal,
born to die with the enlarged hearts of athletes at forty—
Abraham sired with less expectancy,
heaven his friend, the earth his follower.

For John Berryman 2
    (JANUARY, AFTER HIS DEATH)
Your Northwest and my New England are hay and ice;
winter in England's still green out of season,
here the night comes by four. *When will I see you,*
John? You flash back brightly to my mind,
a net too grandly woven to catch the fry.
Brushbeard, the Victorians waking looked like you . . .
last Christmas at the Chelsea where Dylan Thomas died—
uninterruptible, high without assurance,
of the gayest cloth and toughly twisted.
"I was thinking through dinner, I'll never see you again."
One year of wild not drinking, three or four books. . . .
Student in essence, once razor-cheeked like Joyce,
jamming your seat in the crew race, bleeding your ass—
suicide, the inalienable right of man.

Last Night

Is dying harder than being already dead?
I came to my first class without a textbook,
saw the watch I mailed my daughter didn't run;
I opened an old closet door, and found myself
covered with quicklime, my face deliquescent . . .
by oversight still recognizable.
Thank God, I was the first to find myself.
Ah the swift vanishing of my older
generation—the deaths, suicide, madness
of Roethke, Berryman, Jarrell and Lowell,
"the last the most discouraging of all
surviving to dissipate *Lord Weary's Castle*
and nine subsequent useful poems
in the seedy grandiloquence of *Notebook*."

Gods of the Family

My high blood less hotly burns its mortal coil,
I could live on, if free to leave the earth—
hoping to find the Greenbeard Giant, and win
springtide's circlet of the fickle laurel—
a wreath for my funeral from the Gallant Gangster.
I feel familiar cycles of pain in my back,
reticulations of the spawning cell,
intimations of our family cancer—
Grandmother's amnesia, Grandfather's cancered face
wincing at my adolescent spots—
with us no husband can survive his wife.
His widow tried to keep him alive by sending
blackbordered letters like stamps from Turkestan.
Where are they? They had three children, horses, Boston.

Red and Black Brick Boston

Life will not extend, though I'm in love;
light takes on meaning any afternoon
now, ten years from now, or yesterday.
The arctic brightness bakes the red bricks black,
a color too chequered to splash its happiness—
the winter sun is shining on something worthy,
begging the visible be eternal.
Eternity isn't love, or made for children;
a man and woman may meet in love though married,
and risk their souls to snatch a child's attention.
I glow with the warmth of these soiled red bricks,
their unalikeness in similarity,
a senseless originality for fact,
"Rome was," we told the Irish, "Boston is."

Death and the Bridge

(FROM A LANDSCAPE BY FRANK PARKER)
Death gallops on a bridge of red railties and girder,
a onetime view of Boston humps the saltmarsh;
it is handpainted: this the eternal, provincial
city Dante saw as Florence and hell. . . .
On weekends even, the local TV station's
garbage disposer starts to sing at daybreak:
keep Sunday clean. We owe the Lord too much;
from the first, God squared His socialistic conscience,
gave universal capital punishment.
The red scaffolding relaxes and almost breathes:
no man is ever too good to die. . . .
We will follow our skeletons on the girder,
out of life and Boston, singing with Freud:
"God's ways are dark and very seldom pleasant."

Outlook

On my rainy outlook, the great shade is up,
my window, five feet wide, is raised a foot,
most of the view is blanked by brick and windows.
Domestic gusts of noonday Sunday cooking;
black snow grills on the fire-escape's blacker iron,
like the coal that touched Isaiah's unclean tongue. . . .
I hear dead sounds ascending, the fertile stench
of horsedroppings from the war-year of my birth.
Since our '17, how many millions gone—
this same street, West Sixty-Seven, was here,
and this same building, the last gasp of true,
Nineteenth Century Capitalistic Gothic—
horsedroppings and drippings . . . hear it, hear the clopping
hundreds of horses unstopping . . . each hauls a coffin.

Memorial Day

Sometimes I sink a thousand centuries
bone tired then stone-asleep . . . to sleep ten seconds—
voices, the music students, the future voices,
go crowding through the chilling open windows,
fathomless profundities of inanition:
I will be dead then as the dead die here . . .
dáda, dáda dáda dá dá.
But nothing will be put back right in time,
done over, thought through straight for once—not my father
revitalizing in a simple Rhineland spa,
to the beat of Hitler's misguiding roosterstep. . . .
Ah, ah, this house of twenty-foot apartments,
all all windows, yawning—the voice of the student singer's
Don Giovanni fortissimo sunk in the dead brick.

Ice

Iced over soon; it's nothing; we're used to sickness;
too little perspiration in the bucket—
in the beginning, polio once a summer. Not now;
each day the cork more sweetly leaves the bottle,
except a sudden falseness in the breath. . . .
Sooner or later the chalk wears out the smile,
and angrily we skate on blacker ice,
playthings of the current and cold fish—
the naught is no longer asset or disadvantage,
our life too long for comfort and too brief
for perfection—Cro-Magnon, dinosaur . . .
the neverness of meeting nightly like surgeons'
apprentices studying their own skeletons,
old friends and mammoth flesh preserved in ice.

End of a Year

These conquered kings pass furiously away;
gods die in flesh and spirit and live in print,
each library a misquoted tyrant's home.
A year runs out in the movies, must be written
in bad, straightforward, unscanning sentences—
stamped, trampled, branded on backs of carbons,
lines, words, letters nailed to letters, words, lines—
the typescript looks like a Rosetta Stone. . . .
One more annus mirabilis, its hero *hero demens*,
ill-starred of men and crossed by his fixed stars,
running his ship past sound-spar on the rocks. . . .
The slush-ice on the east bank of the Hudson
is rose-heather in the New Year sunset;
bright sky, bright sky, carbon scarred with ciphers.